Florida Folktales

UNIVERSITY PRESSES OF FLORIDA

University of Florida Press / Gainesville

FLORIDA
FOLKTALES

edited by
J. Russell Reaver

UNIVERSITY PRESSES OF FLORIDA is the central agency for scholarly publishing of the State of Florida's university system, producing books selected for publication by the faculty editorial committees of Florida's nine public universities: Florida A&M University (Tallahassee), Florida Atlantic University (Boca Raton), Florida International University (Miami), Florida State University (Tallahassee), University of Central Florida (Orlando), University of Florida (Gainesville), University of North Florida (Jacksonville), University of South Florida (Tampa), University of West Florida (Pensacola).

ORDERS for books published by all member presses of University Presses of Florida should be addressed to University Presses of Florida, 15 NW 15th Street, Gainesville FL 32603.

Library of Congress Cataloging-in-Publication Data

Florida folktales.

   Bibliography: p.
   Includes indexes.
   1. Tales—Florida.   I. Reaver, J. Russell
(Joseph Russell), 1915–
GR110.F5F57   1988   398.2'09759   87-14259
ISBN 0-8130-0870-0 (alk. paper)

Linoleum prints by Larry Leshan

For my Florida friends

With many fond memories, I return your lore to you. It's yours, not mine. Thanks for sharing it with me through the years we've spent together after I got Florida sand in my shoes!

CONTENTS

INTRODUCTION *xi*

1. International Folktales

ANIMAL TALES

1. Clever Fisherman *3*
2. The Stolen Dinner *3*
3. Eyeball Candy *5*
4. The Foolish Diver *5*
5. Learning to Fear Men *6*
6. The Tarbaby *7*

ORDINARY FOLKTALES

7. Learning What Fear Is *10*
8. Katie and Johnnie *10*
9. Outwitting the Giant *11*
10. Old Tor *12*
11. The Witch's Curse *13*
12. Peazy and Beanzy *13*
13. The Milky Way *16*
14. Buried Treasure *16*
15. Dividing the Crops *17*
16. Chopping Off a Head *18*

JOKES AND ANECDOTES

17. The Vengeful Corpse *20*
18. The Lucky Shot *21*
19. The Continual Liar *21*
20. The Land of the Lazy *21*
21. Larger than Life *22*

2. Legends

22. Origin of Seminole Clans and Black People *25*
23. The Flood *25*
24. The Giants of Florida *26*
25. Origin of Spanish Moss *27*
26. Origins of Seminole Indian Food *28*
27. Origin of Hushpuppies *28*
28. Origin of Packenham's Rum
    (The Corpse in the Cask) *29*
29. Early St. Augustine *30*

30. José Gaspar *32*
31. The Dark Nights in May *35*
32. The She-Man *36*
33. Choosing the Site for the State Capitol *39*
34. Legendary Tallahassee *40*
35. Lost at Sea *50*
36. Tallahassee Houses *50*
37. The Last Tallahassee Indians *52*
38. Wakulla Pocahontas *52*
39. Chief Tom Tiger *53*
40. The Skeleton in the Tree *54*
41. The Runaway Slave *55*
42. Blood on the Floor *57*
43. Capture by the "Enemy" *57*
44. The Headless Horseman *58*
45. The Haunted Kissimmee River *59*
46. Uncle Ben Yates *60*
47. Arcadia Heroes *61*
48. Wacissa Folks *64*
49. Cursed Clock *66*
50. Family Friends *66*
51. Hunting the Christmas Baby *71*
52. The Mummy Lover *72*
53. Foreknowledge of Death *73*

3. *Tall Tales and Trickster Stories*

54. Tall Tales *77*
55. More Stretchers *80*
56. The Connoisseur's Sensitive Taste *82*
57. The Right Platform for the Republican Party *83*
58. Putting His Foot in His Mouth *83*
59. Courting Problems *84*
60. Golden Wedding Anniversary *84*
61. Stolen Camellias *85*
62. The Stolen Bus Ticket *85*
63. The Good Baptist *86*
64. Traditional Rivals *86*
65. The Gluke Maker *87*

4. *Ghost Tales and Horror Stories*

66. Self-Burial *91*
67. Buried Alive *91*
68. The Living Corpse *92*
69. Saved from Live Burial *92*

70. The Tallahassee Witch *92*
71. The Haunted Jail *94*
72. The Music Lover *95*
73. The Face on the Windowpane *96*
74. Room for One More *96*
75. The Fraternity Initiation *97*
76. Effects from a Skylight *97*
77. The Cadaver Arm *99*
78. The Wife Who Wouldn't Wear Pants *99*
79. White Visitor to Cemetery *100*
80. The Bewitched Cow *100*
81. Anamoses and Truenina *101*
82. Respect for Ghosts *103*
83. Specters, Spirits, and Souls *104*

5. *Urban Belief Tales*

84. The Roasted Cat *113*
85. The Concrete-filled Cadillac *113*
86. The Choking Doberman *113*
87. The Dead Cat in the Grocery Sack *113*
88. The Surprise in the Elevator *114*
89. Multiple Thefts *114*
90. Treacherous Snakes *115*

NOTES *117*

SELECTED BIBLIOGRAPHY *163*

INDEX OF MOTIFS *166*

INDEX OF TALE TYPES *178*

INTRODUCTION

Collecting Florida Lore

Ever since I got Florida sand in my shoes many years ago, I have been sharing lore with Florida folks. I first became aware of Floridians' sense of place and tradition when as a youngster playing on the St. Augustine beach I heard a city resident say that St. Augustine was the real center of Florida; people just sent their troubles to Tallahassee. Several years later, when I came to live in Tallahassee, I realized it was not only a place for politicians in the state buildings or professors on the university campuses but also a place of rich traditions among the folks of north Florida. Their beliefs and customs and ways of speaking, their tales and legends gave me a sense of what Florida meant to them. Over thirty years of living in Florida have perhaps given me the right to feel I am an adopted son.

What Florida means to me now is Addie Smith telling me about her life on the Brighton Indian Reservation, particularly her interpreting the day of "scratching" before the Seminole Green Corn Dance, when the men's bodies would be purified by drawing their blood with snake fangs or needles. Florida means black folks telling about "Diddy-Wah-Diddy," where they can sit on curbstones and eat all they want from the baked chicken or sweet potato pie as it passes before them.

Florida is Prince Murat living on his plantation, where he refused to remove his shoes until they wore out, or Tampa's Cat Man, who lived as a hermit on his barge in the bay, surrounded by roaming cats. Other memories cluster around the Camino del Rey, or the King's Road, from New Smyrna to Cow Ford, the early site of Jacksonville; E. L. Reyes, a retired Minorcan from Moultrie, told me of adventures along that old trail. Florida is the family legend of all the storytellers, black and white, who vouch for their family history—as Mattie Plummer said, she never "cotched her granddaddy in no lie." Florida brought me Aunt Rachel's explanation of the origin of hushpuppies; after I published the story, it became the basis of a General Mills ad for hushpuppy mix.

Florida is the Snake Woman living along the Suwannee River. Her son left home too soon, without learning her lore, and died from a rattlesnake bite in a swamp, where he was lying near rattlesnake plantain leaves that could have saved his life.

Jesters, tricksters, strongmen, thieves, self-sacrificing

women, gossiping neighbors, hermits, eccentrics, heroes, villains, saints, and sinners are all part of the Florida land where they lived out their lives among the sand dunes or swamps, the oak-covered hills or bottomless sinkholes, the citrus groves or the fishing docks.

Florida is towns, counties, farms, lakes, bays, gulfs, rivers, swamps, woods, beaches, hills, and the long, fantastic coastline that some Seminoles say the white swan created when it riled up the ocean bed to provide a safe retreat for Good Twin to escape the cold blasts of Evil Twin. Spanish moss can mean the greying beard of a Spanish sailor; and the bright, poisonous orange blossoms on a Geiger tree warn me never to pick them and bring them home.

Florida to me is all its people and the tales they tell—for example, Mose Miles, acting out the part of Brer Rabbit when he was swatting the Tarbaby. Mr. Miles's original tale of "Eye-Ball Candy," a treasure of black story-telling, was so admired by J. Mason Brewer that he published it in his collection, *American Negro Folklore*.

Staying with the hospitable Spencer family of Okaloosa County at their home in Laurel Hill, I became acquainted with a whole community of bearers of local legends about Indian raids, the railroad days, haunted houses and ghost-filled caves between Laurel Hill and Florala, Alabama—even though one storyteller could not sing me his old ballads as freely as he would have liked because his Baptist wife thought they were sinful.

Other friends told me about the She-Man of the Caloosahatchee River and the pirates on Gasparilla Island, as well as Acrefoot Johnson, Zeba King, and Bone Mizelle, famous in the cattle country around Arcadia. One delightful old lady introduced herself to me as the daughter Mary of the man who made up the town name of Wimauma from parts of his daughters' names: Wilma, Maude, and Mary.

Key West reminds me both of George Key's weird legend of the mummified Cuban girl kept in her physician's bed and of Nancy Watkins's beautiful story of the indigo-blue stream of the "Black Bottomless Waters," coursing through the turquoise and emerald of the Gulf Stream; at this spot it always rains when a boat crosses, so the fishermen and shrimpers avoid it and go the long way round because they feel it's better to get home late than not to get home at all.

Now I know that when Floridians say, "Give me a Yankee

dime and a Dutch nickel," they mean a kiss and a big hug, and they are praising someone extravagantly when they are "building him up higher than a cat's back." Floridians believe in self-reliance, proclaiming that "Every tub has to sit on its own bottom." They are not discussing farming when they remark that "It's too wet to plow" but are feeling that the situation is past helping. Although I have eaten possum with Florida natives, they are likely to mean they regret some other action when they confess, "I wish I hadn't et that possum."

Thanks to Lucy Kalogera, I am familiar with the superstitions of shrimp fishermen in the Panacea-Apalachicola areas, who will not allow a sea turtle, dead or alive, or even the empty turtle shell, to touch the deck of a shrimp boat, because it will hex the boat. I know that if my cat ever has the blind staggers from eating lizards, all I need to do is follow the advice of Betsy Woods and dig up the rhizome of a nettle, mash it after cooking it in milk, and serve it to my suffering pet. When I go to the dog racing track at Miami, I can always win if a ticket seller punches out a wrong number, for Walter Pearcey has told me it's a sign of good luck at dog races. And I can treat with particular respect the Seminole Indian who let me know that if he puts a curse on a feather it will fly to his enemy's camp, and every night it will draw blood from him, filling its hollow quill, until he dies.

I can now entertain children with W. D. Grovenstein's West Palm Beach tales of Katie and Johnnie outwitting their giant captor or of Jack tricking the giant into believing that the bird he lets fly from his hand is really a stone that he can throw until it disappears. Or I can amuse youngsters with Robert Woll's rhymes from Wewahitchka:

Joe, Joe broke his toe
On his way to Mexico.
On his way back
He broke his back
Sliding on a railroad track.

Or I can recite to my older friends:

An epicure dining at Crew
Found quite a large mouse in his stew.
Said the waiter, "Don't shout and wave it about,
Or the rest will be wanting one too!"

But after all these years spent learning the tales, legends, myths, customs, speech, rhymes, and sayings of my Florida friends, perhaps the most welcome advice came from George, the Key West taxi driver, who once told me that if I ate conch chowder I would never die but would live to be so old that I would just dry up and blow away!

These selections from my archive of Florida tales represent five main sorts of storytelling: internationally known stories (animal stories, ordinary folktales, and jokes and anecdotes); popular legends; tall tales and trickster stories; ghost tales and horror stories; and urban belief tales.

Chapter 1, "International Folktales," is arranged according to the three categories in the Aarne-Thompson index of tale types: Animal Tales, Ordinary Folktales, and Jokes and Anecdotes.

The first six tales retell classic types of animal stories with the exception of Tale 3, "Eyeball Candy," the apparent invention of Mose Miles, an outstanding teller of tales from north Florida.

The range of ordinary folktales in oral circulation is indicated by the local variants of "Hansel and Gretel," "Sleeping Beauty," and "The Kind and the Unkind Girls," among several others.

Tales of the vengeful corpse and the coffin maker as well as the joys of "Schlaraffenland," the heaven of the lazy, represent Florida jokes and anecdotes, along with some instances of the tall tale.

Chapter 2 presents in a more or less chronological order a wide range of popular legends, from the creation stories of Seminole Indians and black people to stories about the Second World War and contemporary university life. Such legends reveal the popular history of Floridians who remember the past as they wish it had been.

The trickster tales of chapter 3 still amuse many, whether they are stories to fool the greenhorn—typical of pioneering life on the frontier—or stories of more modern vintage in which the trickster not only plays tricks on others but at times tricks himself. Some Florida tricksters have been immortalized as comic heroes.

Ghost tales, in the fourth chapter, allow listeners to experience vicariously the horrors described by the storyteller. Nearly equal in popularity to the trickster tales, these thrillers continue to excite the imaginations of Florida folks.

The urban belief tales in chapter 5 have only recently been

included in the canon of folktales. Most of them draw upon the same kinds of trickery or horror that make the earlier comic or ghost tales entertaining; but the jesting in these modern accounts of big city life is tempered by the insecurity and fear caused by the complexities and tensions of metropolitan living.

Notes on the tale texts give information about informants, analogues to Florida tales (especially the international types), and the classification of tale types and identification of pertinent motifs in each text.

The bibliography lists principal books and articles referred to in the notes, with aids to further study. The indexes summarize motifs and tale types, indicating the broad range of subjects in Florida folktales, their relations to other groups of motifs or types mentioned in the notes, and displaying their locations in this volume according to tale number and corresponding note number.

The collection is entitled *Florida Folktales*, in keeping with Richard M. Dorson's use of the generic term for books in the series *Folktales of the World* (University of Chicago Press). This practice follows the wisdom of Stith Thompson, who advised scholars that the word *folktale* not only may be applied to the *fairy tale*, which the Germans know as the *Märchen*, but "it is also legitimately employed in a much broader sense to include all forms of prose narrative, written or oral, which have come to be handed down through the years. In this usage the important fact is the traditional nature of the material" (*The Folktale* [New York, 1946], p. 4). For instance, in organizing traditional British narratives for *Folktales of England*, Katherine M. Briggs used such categories as Wonder Tales, Legends, and Jocular Tales, with numerous subdivisions suggesting either the subjects of such narratives or the audience for whom they were intended.

Scholars may continue to debate about their methods for classifying tales, just as they still argue about their choices for identifying motifs and types within storytelling traditions. But to the people who tell stories such fine distinctions do not exist. In this collection some stories are classified by the method of cataloging used in the Aarne-Thompson *Type-Index*, generally satisfactory for Anglo-American narratives. The category "Legends" appears mainly because it suggests a quasi-historical association; yet the associations aroused by certain narratives may vary among storytellers and their audience. Katherine Briggs interprets degrees of historical truth attached to legends:

Broadly speaking, one may say that legends are tales or anecdotes told as fact, often about particular places or people, or about friends of the narrator, or his friends' friends. Thus they are distinguished from other folktales of all kinds, which are told for entertainment or edification, with only a playful pretense of being factual. This distinction is clear in the main, but it does not necessarily affect the shape of the story. Exactly the same story might be told by two men, one of whom believed it and recorded it as a fact while the other told it purely as a good tale. A further difficulty is that it seems likely that legends of the origin of local features—standing stones and mounds and the like—were never really believed at all, but were playful exercises of imagination. (*Folktales of England* [Chicago: University of Chicago Press, 1965], pp. xxvi–xxvii)

The narratives in *Florida Folktales* form part of the remembered past in many sections of the state; many are directly quoted. They range from the oral tales of Mose Miles, who could neither read nor write and thought all his stories were his own inventions, through the legends about José Gaspar remembered in Alice Welch's family of local historians along the Gulf coast, to recent urban stories I have heard from college professors who half-believe them. E. L. Reyes had already written down his recollections of St. Augustine before I met him in 1950; he kept them in his backyard shed among family antiques and had reread them so often he could recite them almost word for word. I learned the story of the origin of hushpuppies purely by accident when I happened to question Aunt Rachel about her recipe. My account of the mysterious witch's burial resulted from incidental talks with visitors of her grave, including one young man who places flowers there on her birthday. Some accounts became my own way of remembering the past of local friends, like the story of the Florida giants; the fullest narrative came from Ed Bell, but he had heard other versions too. Students sometimes became bridges to their families. As conditions allowed, a tape recorder or notebook came in handy; occasionally scrapbooks and family papers provided help. The common thread in all these methods has been my effort to remain faithful to the goal of revealing the Florida known only through its many tellers of tales.

O N E

International Folktales

ANIMAL TALES

1. Clever Fisherman

"I'll tell you about Buh Gator fust. Well, Buh Rabbit come 'long one mornin'. Buh Gator was layin' down by the pond. Buh Rabbit had been down to the pond. Buh Gator, he was up on the hillside from the pond layin' out in a straw field.

"Buh Gator said to Buh Rabbit, 'Say, Buh Rabbit, where you get so many fishes?'

"He said, 'Oh, I went down there to the lake and ketch 'em this mornin'.'

" 'Well, how did you ketch 'em?'

" 'Oh,' he said, 'I just went down there and broke the ice and stuck mah tail in the wawtah, and when I pulled it up I had a bunch o' fish.'

"He said, 'Dat so?' "

2. The Stolen Dinner

Variant A

"Aunt Mary's husband, Uncle George, ya know, dis happen t' him back dere in slavery time. Uncle George he was a 'possum hunter. One night he got him a 'possum an' he dress 'im all down, but fo' he eat 'im he got t' sleep wif de 'possum cookin' in de pot.

"Three li'l boys dey come in an' eat de 'possum while ol' Uncle George sleep. Den dey put de 'possum grease all 'roun' ol' Uncle George mouf.

"Ol' Uncle George woke up an' he raise sand 'bout somebody done eat up his 'possum. But de boys dey bro't in a mirror an' show Uncle George his mouf all greased-up like, an' Uncle George say, 'Well, boys, I sho' did eat dat 'possum. I mus' a been so sleepy I didn' eben know I eat him.' "

Variant B

"Well, ya know, Buh Rabbit and Buh Fox, they was farmin' together. And so, they were workin'. Buh Rabbit, he was married. Buh Fox wasn't. So they was workin' not far from the house. So dey cooked a dinner so dey wouldn't have to cook dat at twelve o'clock.

"Once in a while Buh Rabbit stopped, and Buh Fox say, 'Who dat, Buh Rabbit?'

"He say, 'Now, my wife callin' me to da house.'

" 'What she want?'

" 'I don' know.'

" 'Go dere an' see what she want.'

"Buh Rabbit, he go to da house.

"Well, he'd eat so much he want right den. Go back. He'd work a little bit more and stop.

"Buh Fox'd say, 'Hey, who dat callin' you, Buh Rabbit?'

" 'My wife callin' me to da house.'

" 'What she want?'

" 'I don' know.'

" 'Go see what she want.'

"He'd go back, eat a little bit more. He'd go on back, work about a row or so.

" 'I wish that woman would quit callin' me, I'm so tired of her I don't know what in the world to do.'

" 'Well, go see what she want, Buh Rabbit.'

"Buh Rabbit went on back.

"Well, twelve o'clock come, he knocked off for dinner. He went dere, and nothin' t' eat. All right: was gone.

"Buh Fox said to Buh Rabbit, 'Buh Rabbit!'

" 'Hey!'

" 'You know they ain't a thing at dinner.'

" 'Well, I don't know what become of it, Buh Fox, 'cause hit was here when I come in.'

" 'Didn't you eat it, Buh Rabbit?'

" 'No, no, I ain't had my hand on it.'

" 'Well, I know what I'm goin' do. And the one what et it, I'll find out. I'm gonna make up a big fire, and make 'um jump over dat fire, and da one dat can't jump over it, and fall in, dat's da man et it.'

"Buh Fox, he made up a big fire. Well, den he comes to jumping. Buh Rabbit, he git way back, he take a runnin' start. 'Stead of he jumpin' over, he go 'round. The rest'd go over. Well, they tried an' tried.

" 'Oh, you went 'round that time, Buh Rabbit.'

" 'No, I went over it, I went over it. Now, you watch me now.'

"He'd go way back, he'd take a runnin' start, run up to the fire and go right around it.

"And so, Buh Fox said, 'Buh Rabbit, you et that.' "

3. Eyeball Candy

"And so, after dat den, Buh Fox come along one day. (Dis about Buh Rabbit ag'in.) Buh Rabbit had some just little round ball candy. (He called it eyeball candy). He come on up dere where Buh Fox was.

"Buh Fox, he said, 'Buh Rabbit!'

"He said, 'Uh huh.'

" 'What dat you eatin'?'

" 'Oh, man, dis somp'un good. You wanna taste it?'

" 'Yeah! I wanna taste it.'

"So he let him taste a piece of candy. And Buh Fox taste it.

"He say, 'What you call it?'

" 'Eyeball candy.'

"Buh Fox said, 'Reckon if I pull out one of my eyes, it'd eat like dis?'

"He said, 'Oh, man, yeah! yeah! It'd eat like dat, sho!'

"So he let Buh Rabbit pull one of his eyeballs out. Buh Rabbit took some of the candy and just smeared it all over the eyeball to make it taste sweet, ya know.

"So when he got it, well, dat taste all right to Buh Fox!

"Buh Fox said, 'Pull out the other one!'

"When he pulled out de other one, den he called da hounds, said, 'Hyah, hyah, hyah!'

"And Buh Fox just tore out there and just butt his fat head on 'gainst the tree.

"Buh Rabbit just slick to death!"

4. The Foolish Diver

Variant A

"Buh Rabbit wuz tryin' t' git some water fum de well 'cause he sho' wuz thirsty. He leaned over a little too far an' fell in. They wuz a bucket at de bottom of de well but Buh Rabbit couldn' get out 'cause they wasn't nuthin' t' pull 'im up. He stayed dere all day 'til the moon come out dat night.

"Bout dat time ol' Buh Fox come by an' saw Buh Rabbit in de well. He say, 'W'atcha doin' way down 'ere?'

"Buh Rabbit say he was jes' down 'ere eatin' cheese ('cause de moon look like a big round yella' cheese down 'ere in de water).

"Buh Fox, he say, 'How 'bout me comin' down 'ere an' gettin' some o' dat cheese?'

"Buh Rabbit, he say, 'Sho, come on down,' 'cause he knowed that wid all dat weight Buh Fox would sho haul him up.

"So Buh Fox come on down an' when Buh Rabbit got to de top he jumped outta de bucket an' say:

" 'Goodbye, brother Fox, you will get dere soon; fast on cheese wid de man in de moon.' "

Variant B

"Buh Rabbit was drawin' at one o' dese yeah open wells one day an' he got carried down to de bottom of de well an' he couldn' get up ag'in!

"Well, ol' Buh Fox, he come by an' he seed Buh Rabbit down deah in de well.

"He say, 'Hey dere, Buh Rabbit, what you doin' in dat well?'

"An' Buh Rabbit, he say, 'Oh, I comes down heah 'most every day 'bout dis time fo' a nice drink o' water.'

"So Buh Fox, he say, 'How 'bout me comin' down deah fo' a drink too?'

"Buh Rabbit, he say, 'Sho, Buh Fox, you come on down,' 'cause he knowed de fox wuz heavier dan 'e wuz an' would git 'im outta dat well.

"Buh Fox, he got in de bucket an', while he was goin' down, Buh Rabbit was comin' up an' he say, 'Yassuh, Buh Fox, I'm goin' an' you is comin'! Dat's de way de world goes, some goin' an' some comin'!' "

5. *Learning to Fear Men*

"It used to be that whenever dey was any preachers come to visit on the farm, they used t' kill two-three chickens, mebbe a turkey or two, o' sunthin' to feed 'em. It got t' where all de chickens an' turkeys could tell de preachers mos' any time dey come, an' dey would take to de swamp.

"One day dey was three preachers come visitin', and o' co'se all de chickens an' de ducks, an' de roosters, an' de turkeys an' guineas took t' de swamp t' hide 'til dose preachers lef'!

"De fust one t' pop out de swamp t' see if dose preachers done lef' was de ol' rooster. He say, 'Preachers all gone?' [Here the narrator imitated a rooster.]

"De guinea say, 'Not yet, not yet.'

"De duck say, 'Shh, shh.'

"Den de rooster he say again, 'Preachers all gone?'

"An' de ol' turkey gobbler say, 'Coupla de scoun'els, coupla de scoun'els.' "

6. The Tarbaby

"Dis about Buh Rabbit and Buh Fox right on.

"So, dey had a spring, and all of 'um usin' well wawtah out da same well. So da spring got low in wawtah like is usable.

"So—Buh Rabbit, he'd go dere soon in da mornin', and git his wawtah, and he'd jump in da spring and muddy it all up.

"Buh Fox didn't understand dat. He kept goin'. And he asked one day, 'Ho, Buh Rabbit!'

"Buh Rabbit say, 'Hey!'

" 'Why da wawtah bein' so muddy when I goes dere? How do *you* gits wawtah?'

"He says, 'I don' know why dat wawtah bein' muddy. Twan't muddy when I went dere.'

"He say, 'Well, ever' mornin' I go dere, dat wawtah bein' muddy, and I can' understand it, so I'm goin' see 'bout it.'

"So Buh Rabbit, he kep' on. Buh Fox, he wouldn't make no outcry.

"So Buh Fox makes 'im a tarbaby. (So—Buh Rabbit, he da one muddyin' da wawtah.) So he sot it to da well. So dat mornin' Buh Rabbit went dere.

"He says, 'Uh!'

"He went dere to da well. He looked at da baby. He looked at da thing.

"He say, 'Good evenin', Ma'am!'

"She wouldn't said nothin'.

"Said, 'Good evenin', Ma'am!'

"She wouldn't said nothin'.

"Said, 'Now you better speak to me. If you don' speak, I'm gonna slap you head off.'

"Yet she ain't said nothin'.

"He hauled back and slapped her.

"That time Buh Rabbit said, 'I got another hand here. You better turn me loose! You better turn me loose! I got another hand, if I gotta wait 'til I slap you down!'

"And so, he hauled back and slapped the tarbaby wid dat hand. Well, dat un' stuck.

"He said, 'Please, Ma'am, turn me loose. Please, Ma'am, turn me loose.'

"B' yet she ain't said nothin'.

"He said, 'I got a foot yere, I know what I'll do: 'f I'll kick you, you'll sure turn me loose.'

"He hauled back and kicked her with his foot. Well, that foot stuck.

"He said, 'Turn me loose! I got a nother un' here and I know 'f I'll kick ya wid this un' I'll kill ya.'

"He hauled back and kicked her wid dat foot. Well, all dem stuck.

"Dat time he say, 'I got a head here, an' now I'll butt ya, an' if I butt ya, I'll kill ya.'

"He butted her. Dat time de head stuck.

"Dat time da fox walked up.

" 'Uh huh, Buh Rabbit, you da very one been doin' dat wawtah!'

"No, Buh Fox, no! God know, Buh Fox, it 'twan't me. I just come dere, and somebody was here, an' I tryin' to fin' out dat's da one been muddyin' da wawtah. An I got at 'um, an' I got stuck. Please, Buh Fox, turn me loose!'

"He said, 'No, I ain't gone turn ya loose.'

"He took Buh Rabbit den, got 'im by all 'is foots.

"He said, 'Well, I got a good mind to throw you in the well and kill ya.'

"He said, 'No, don't throw me in the well. Please, don't throw me in the well. I'd rather y'd do anything to me than throw me in the well.'

"Buh Fox looked all 'round then to see the thickest briar patch he could find.

" 'Now I know what I'm goin' do. I goin' throw you in dat briar patch over yondah.'

" 'Please, Buh Fox, don't throw me in the briar patch, don't throw me in the briar patch!'

"Buh Fox went on, took him by the foots, carried him on through the thickest briar patch, throwed 'im over in the briar patch.

" 'Whoa, oh, ho, by God, I been bred and born dere!'

ORDINARY FOLKTALES

7. *Learning What Fear Is*

"An old slavery-time Negro who once lived on my father's farm told me this story when I was a child.

"Lawd, chile, did I ever tell you 'bout de time when I wuz scared 'most to deff? Well, I wuz goin' thu de woods over by Miz Anders' house when I heered sompin' behind me. It sounded like somebody walkin'. Well, it was late at night an' them wuz lonesome woods. I had been settin' up wid Mr. Anders. He wuz sick. I turned my head jus' a little and outta de corner ob my eye I saw de biggest black cat I done ever seed in my life. He wuz walkin' on his hind legs jus' like a human. He looked at me an' grinned. I didn' take time to grin back. I jus' lit out. I run an' run 'til I give out. Then I drop down on a log to res'. That cat wuz settin' dar right 'side me. He look at me wid dem eyes red as coals ob fire an' he say, "Ain' nobody here but me an' you tonight." I said, "No, an' dey ain' goin' be nobody but you in a minute."

" 'I lit a rag ag'in. I run an' I run 'til I couldn't run no mo'. I fell down 'side a branch. Dere wuz dat cat right 'side me. He said de same thing to me, and I jump up and run some mo'.

" 'If I hadn' got to a frien's house soon I woulda dropped dead. Dey say dey ain' see no cat, but I know he wuz wid me all de way dere. Where he come frum an' where he go, I don' know.'

"And old Uncle Pomp would shake his head and chuckle and look at my puzzled face."

8. *Katie and Johnnie*

"One time there was a little boy and a little girl, brother and sister, who lived on a farm in Georgia. Their names were Katie and Johnnie. Their mother told them to go down in the woods and get some switches to make brooms with and sweep both the back and the front yards. This seemed an awful task to Katie and Johnnie since you know backyards in South Georgia cover at least an acre.

"Katie and Johnnie left for the woods and found some gall-berry bushes for brooms.

"Johnny said, 'Let's go down in the swamp a little further,' and Katie agreed.

"Pretty soon Katie said, 'What's that?'

"Johnnie looked over and saw two delicious-looking cakes hanging down from two ropes on the limb of a tree.

"Katie said to Johnnie, 'If you pull one, I'll pull the other.'

"So they did, and about that time down came a big cage and caught those two disobedient kids who had gone farther into the swamp than they were supposed to.

"A big giant came up laughing, 'Ho! Ho! I've got you now!' and carried Katie and Johnnie off squealing.

"He walked—boom, boom, boom—through the forest to his hangout. He gathered up some wood and got an old iron pot to cook the two children in.

"Johnnie said, 'I wonder what that ol' giant's going to do.' He saw the giant getting lightwood knots and saw him strike two stones together—boom, boom—and start a fire.

"He said to Katie, 'I believe that old giant is going to cook us and we've got to get away. When he comes to the cage, you run this way and I'll run that, and we'll get out of this cage.'

"The old giant got the water all hot to boil Katie and Johnnie, and he smacked his lips—smack, smack, smack.

"He opened the cage and growled at the children, 'Come here, you brats.'

"Boy, the hair on those kids' heads began to rise, they were so scared! When the giant tried to grab them, though, Katie ran one way and Johnnie the other. Before the giant knew what was happening, they had gotten out of the cage and locked him in it! The giant roared and roared and it shook the whole woods and sounded like thunder. But Katie and Johnnie tilted the cage with long sticks and rolled him down, down, down, boom-de-boom-de-boom-de-boom, into the river, ka-doosh-a-dow!

"Katie and Johnnie tore out for home as fast as they could go. They got some black gum switches 'cause they thought their mama would spank them for sure, but she was so glad to see them she just hugged and kissed them and didn't whip them that time."

9. Outwitting the Giant

"One day Jack was out walking, and as he walked over a bridge he saw a giant. The giant was a big, boastful fellow, and he told

Jack about all his feats of strength. Jack was a small boy and he decided he would have a little fun and trick that giant.

"The Giant took a rock in his hand and said to Jack, 'See how strong I am. I can squeeze water right out of this rock,' and he did.

"But Jack said, 'Well, that's pretty good, but I'll bet you can't squeeze milk out of a rock.'

"Of course the giant couldn't, and he didn't think Jack could either; but Jack had a piece of cheese in his pocket and he put that next to the rock in his hand while the giant wasn't looking and 'squeezed milk out of a rock.'

"The giant was angry because he thought Jack was stronger than he was, but he said, 'Well, you may be stronger than I am but I betcha you can't throw a rock as far as I can.'

"He picked up a rock and threw it, and it sailed and sailed, out over the water almost out of sight, but not quite.

"Now Jack had a little bird that he could carry in his pocket. While the giant wasn't looking he took the bird out of his pocket and held it in his hand.

"Then he said to the giant, 'Well, you can throw pretty good, but I believe I can beat you.'

"Then he threw the little bird out, and the bird flew away off out of sight. The old giant thought the bird was a rock and that Jack had thrown farther than he had. He went stomping off very angry because Jack was stronger and could throw farther than he could. He never found out how Jack outsmarted him."

10. Old Tor

"One time there was some little boys and girls sitting around the fireplace. They kept cutting up and their mama told them if they didn't be quiet Old Tor would come and get them. Well, they didn't be quiet, and their mama said, 'Old Tor, where are you?' Old dog lying by the fire got up and sniffed at the door.

"A big shadow fell across the room and the mama say, 'Who's that up there?'

"A great big rumble voice say, 'This is Big Tor; I get boys and girls that don't behave.'

"The Mama say, 'What's them big feet for?' (Crack, crack, crack.)

" 'THE BETTER TO WALK WITH!'

"The Mama say, "What's them big legs for?' (Crack, crack, crack.)

" 'THE BETTER TO HOLD MYSELF UP WITH!'

" 'What's them big eyes for?' (Crack, crack, crack.)

" 'THE BETTER TO SEE YOU WITH!'

" 'What's them big hands for?'

" 'THE BETTER TO CATCH YOU WITH!' " "

(Here the storyteller grabs the child. The story may be told as long as the bodily parts hold out. Ears are better to hear with, nose better to smell with, mouth better to eat with, etc.)

11. The Witch's Curse

"Once there was a man and his wife who had eleven sons and no daughters. The couple wanted a girl very badly; so they prayed and prayed. After several years had passed, they gave up hope. But one night, a witch visited them. She told them she'd use her power so that they might have a daughter if they would grant her one wish. The man and his wife agreed, but they were very sad when they heard the witch's wish: they had to agree to give their daughter to her when she reached the age of ten.

"The witch kept her word and the couple had a daughter, who grew to be a pretty little girl. At last the day arrived when the witch came for the child. The parents refused to give her up, and the girl's brothers beat the old witch up. The witch went away screaming, 'The girl will die from a horse's hoof!'

"After that, the parents watched the girl carefully and would allow no horse about their place. One day the girl went walking in the woods. She didn't come and didn't come; so her parents and brothers set out to look for her. They found the little girl lying on the ground dead. She had fallen face down in a hole made by a horse's hoof and strangled to death."

12. Peazy and Beanzy

"Now all you gather 'round 'n' I'll tell you 'bout two li'l childrens which was named Peazy 'n' Beanzy . . . they was sisters. They had a aunt what lived in the far east and they always wanted to go visit 'er. Now Peazy, who was mean and hateful, decided to go first; so one day she started on her way to visit her aunt.

"Pretty soon she came to a brook which was all stopped up with brush and stones. That old brook would just go 'Buzzzz' 'n' 'groowllll' so loud 'cause it couldn't skip along its way. But Peazy wouldn't pay no 'tention; she just stepped over it and went on her way.

"On the other side of the brook was a big ole plum tree that was all bent over 'n' broken down, but would Peazy stop and help it? No, she saw it but just stepped on its branches as she walked 'round.

"Pretty soon she got to her aunt's house, but that aunt didn't wanta keep her long. Peazy was lazy 'n' wouldn't set the table or dust or nuthin'.

"She sez, her aunt sez, 'Peazy, you might as well go home; you don't help out your old seek aunt . . . you don't wash no dishes or do the chores,' she sez.

"Now lazy Peazy was glad to leave. She wasn't gonna stay at her rich aunt's if she was gonna have ta work. So she left and on the way home she got ohh so hungry. Pretty soon she came to the sad ole plum tree and thair—right down in the middle of it—was a little fire and wood all set up, just like a little oven. And there sat a little cake a'bakin'.

" 'Ohhhh,' she sez, 'I'd like some of that cake.' And so Peazy reached down with her hand to get some and 'swooooosh!' came a big black crow a-flying down and picked the whole thing up in its beak . . . just a-flappin' off with it.

"Peazy cried, 'Ohh, I'm so hungry. . . .' And on and on she walked. Then she came along to that ole buzzin' brook and there, all build up on the twigs and rocks was the nicest li'l fire. And right in the middle sat a black fryin' pan. Peazy smelled and smelled something good, then she saw in that skillet some fish a-fryin'. She sez, 'Ummmm, I think I'll just have a piece of that nice fish . . . it look so good.' And just as she reached down, that whole brook came unstopped and the fire 'n' fryin' pan 'n' fish all went floating down that big ditch.

" 'Ohhh me oh my . . . I's so hungry I thinks I's gonna die . . .' 'n' Peazy begins to cry and goes to rubbin' her tummy.

"And finally she gets home, her sides so skinny from hunger that her ribs was a-rubbin' together. An' her mother was so mad at her fer bein' bad to the aunt that she even made her scat up to bed without no supper.

"Next day Beanzy sez, 'Maw, why don' you let me visit

Auntie?' So off goes the secon' sister to see that good ole aunt.

"When she comes to that brook it's stopped up all over ag'in. Beanzy steps right over it. . . . But then she stops 'n' turns 'round and sez, 'Oh, you poor buzzin' brook . . . you wants to run 'n' play like the other li'l brooks, don' you?' So Beanzy pulls loose the sticks 'n' stones that was clutterin' it up; then that brook goes merrily runnin' on.

"Then she comes to that poor plum tree all broke over 'n' she sez, 'Poor tree, you wants to grow tall 'n' straight so you can have lotsa nice fruit, don' you?' So she ties up that bent tree with a strip of material she tore right off her dress 'n' on she goes to see her aunt.

"It was even dark when she got there but she wasn't scared. Beanzy goes right into the kitchen and sez, 'Auntie, what can I do to help you? Can't I set the table or help with the cookin' or somethin'?'

"So all the time Beanzy kept busy helpin' her aunt with the chores 'n' she stayed one week, then two, and finally a whole month was up and she sez to her auntie, she sez, 'Auntie, I have to go home now to my mommy 'cause she needs me to help her too. But I'll come back to see you again soon as I can.'

" 'Youse been a dear li'l child, Beanzy,' she sez. 'You isn't lazy at all like your sister Peazy; so I'm gonna give you this bag of money for your present. You is to take it home for your mommy and for you, but don't give none of it to Peazy, 'cause she's gonna haf' to learn how to earn it by workin' like you already know how.'

"So Beanzy thanks her aunt 'n' starts home. Just like her sister Peazy, she sees a li'l cake baking in the middle of the plum tree, but no big crow takes it from her. She looks up 'n' sees a tiniest li'l hummingbird that comes down 'n' sits on her shoulder and sings the prettiest li'l melody while she eats the cake. 'Ummm, so good!' she sez.

"Then just like Peazy she sees some fish a-fryin' when she gets to the brook, and ummmmm, she gets to eat that too.

"Then Beanzy got home. She wasn't hungry 'cause she'd had so much to eat on the way home, 'n' when she showed her mommy that bag full of money they both just danced a jig and her mommy sez, 'Now ain't you glad I brought you up to be such a unselfish and helpful chile!'

"But mean 'n' hateful Peazy just lay over in the corner a-cryin' and a-kickin' up her heels. . . . Bad girl. . . . Now, don' you chilluns be like her!"

13. The Milky Way

"A long while back the Breathmaker blew his breath toward the sky and made the Milky Way. This white way leads to a city in the west where the Big Cypress Seminoles go when they die. Bad people stay in the ground right where they are buried. Every time you go through the woods and step where a bad person is buried you feel afraid even though the grave is covered over with bushes and trees.

"Good people walk over the Milky Way to a 'city in the western sky.' Animals take the same path when they die. Long ago animals of an Indian—dogs and horses—were killed so they might go with their masters."

14. Buried Treasure

Variant A

"When we got down ten or twelve feet we found a sort of thing like the size of a casket. It was more like that than anything else. It was made out of cement. Mr. Willis was working with us. He got a pick and started a-chopping on that box. It was cement most all the way. Directly it broke through. There was a hole in it about the size of a bucket, but there warn't nothing in it but a lot of long black hair. Don't know what went with it.

"Well, [the convicts] went back to digging. Got down about two more feet we found a box. It was all covered over with gold-colored metal—they said it was copper. We didn't get all the sand off it, but it was just a-shining in the sun. The ground was getting plumb loblolly.

"Now, lawyer Johnston, he just ran over to call Mr. Stansbury. He come a-running.

"Well, the men was in the hole, a-trying to get a rope around that box. The sand was sort of falling down all around the hole. Well, now, Mr. Stansbury, he didn't wait none. He jumped right down on that there box, and that box, it just sunk right on down. Those convicts just shinnied right up that rope, with the sand a-caving in all around them. Mr. Stansbury, he was the last one out. He sure wanted that box. By the time he got to the top, the sand was clean up to his knees. We ain't never seen that box again."

Walter Teate told Gene Nabi that the Wacissa River holds some strange objects. In the western slough of the river there is a large rock resembling a coffin that no one has attempted to investigate. Stories also circulate about three large transparent rocks in the river that can never be seen twice by the same person.

The Wacissa is believed to hold hidden treasure. Several years ago the Brumbley boys went down to the river to search for it. While exploring around Camp Pleasant Island, John Brumbley claims, he "got ahold of the treasure pot," but, in attempting to lift it, he found it was extremely heavy. As he brought the pot up a little, it began to tremble and shake so much that after a struggle John had to turn it loose, and the treasure pot has never been located again.

Local residents think that Indians buried treasure in and around the swamp, because pieces of quartz streaked with gold have been found in the Indian mounds. In addition, the old-timers know that Chief Tallahassee comes periodically to visit the Wacissa. Where? Why? No one knows. Yet everyone strongly believes that something in the swamp is worth his making the trip.

15. *Dividing the Crops*

"Buh Rabbit said, 'Well, I'm goin' tell you what I do.' He said, 'Now, I'm goin' try you 'gain. Goin' plant some potatoes and pinders [peanuts].'

"And Buh Rabbit: 'Now, all under the ground, Buh Fox, will be yourn, and all on top be mine.'

"Well, when the taters made, Buh Rabbit, he found out when they was made; so he'd go there at night and he'd dig 'em and eat 'em. Go to the pinder bush and get the pinders that night and eat 'em. So when they got ready to dig potatoes and pinders, well, Buh Fox ain't had nothin' but just the naked bush. Buh Rabbit had done got 'em all. And all that was under the ground was Buh Fox's. And Buh Rabbit had done got 'em.

"And so, Buh Fox said, 'Buh Rabbit, you know somebody done dug dem taters. Who you reckon dug 'em?'

" 'I don' know. I sure ain't dug 'em. I sure ain't dug 'em, Buh Fox.'

"He said, 'Buh Rabbit, I b'lieve you dug dem taters.'

" 'I sure ain't dug 'em. I didn't dig 'em.'

"He said, 'Now, the way to do, you go back there an' dig 'em up, plough 'em up.

"Buh Fox said, 'Dere ain't none under dere!' Buh Rabbit said, 'Well. . . .' He studied, he studied. He said, 'Well, I don't know what become . . . I don't know what become. . . .' He say, 'Oh, I 'member, gran'pa and gran'ma dug dem taters!' "

16. Chopping Off a Head

"Another time Brer Rabbit an' Brer Rooster been friends for long while. Dey had a farm together. Dey was share croppers.

"Oncet was a cold, cold mornin', but Brer Rooster was up early to crow an' wake everybody up. He was sittin' on a fence just a-shiverin' an' a-shakin' with his head tucked under his wing to keep out o' the wind.

"He looked up an' saw Brer Rabbit a-hoppin' 'long da field, an' he thought he'd play a good joke on 'im. So he sits up real straight 'cept his head bein' tucked under his wing.

"Brer Rabbit sez, 'Good mornin', Brer Rooster! Where's your head?'

" 'Oh, I left my head at the house for my lady to have combed for me when I gets back to da house for breakfast.'

" 'What?' sez Brer Rabbit. 'You chopped yo' head off to leave with yo' lady to comb?'

" 'Shore did, Brer Rabbit. Dat saves time an' effort.'

"So Brer Rabbit 'cides he'll have his lady keep his head at home for awhile so she can comb his ears and pick out the burrs.

"Off he runs, clippety-clop, clippety-clop, to his wife.

"He gets da axe an' says, 'Here, chicken, take dis here axe an' chop off my head!'

" 'Chop off your head? You fool, what you talkin' about?'

" 'I said chop off my head like Brer Rooster's is. I wants you to keep it here an' comb the burrs off,' sez Brer Rabbit to his wife.

" 'You fool, you'll be dead!' Miz Rabbit screams.

" 'No I won't. I just saw Brer Rooster, an' he ain't got no head an' he's as live as you. Now chop it off quick, I tell you. Cut dat head off!'

"So Miz Rabbit chops Brer Rabbit's head clean off, an' he just hops 'round a couple times, den fall over flat on his face—I mean, his neck. He is dead as a doornail.

"Den Brer Rooster gets to own da whole farm, an' both his wife an' Brer Rabbit's wife, an' he is *sooo* happy!"

JOKES AND ANECDOTES

17. The Vengeful Corpse

"Once upon a time there was an old man who lived in a little village where he was the undertaker. It got so cold during every winter that the ground froze and the undertaker couldn't bury anyone until spring when the ground thawed out; so during the winter he stored all the bodies that had died during the winter in a little house near the graveyard.

"One winter two men of the town died about the same time. One man was a rich man who was mean and everyone disliked him. The other man was poor but good and everyone loved him. The undertaker decided to switch their caskets so the poor man could have a nicer casket.

"He stored them in the house near the graveyard, and one day he had to go out there for something. While he was in the house, the door blew shut and couldn't be unlocked from the inside. There was a little window in the ceiling of the house which a man could easily go through; so the undertaker piled the caskets up to climb on them and reach the window. When he piled them up, the poor man's casket, in which lay the rich man, was on top. The undertaker climbed up the caskets, and just as he stepped on the top and got his head through the window, the casket fell through and his feet fell into the casket. He let out a horrible cry and fell down the roof onto the ground.

"His scream scared his horse and the horse ran into town. The town doctor noticed the empty saddled horse and sensed that something was wrong; so he went out to the house and found the undertaker. He rushed him to a hospital, where a doctor saw that the bottom of his legs had big gashes in them.

"The doctor decided to go back and see what had caused these gashes. He unpiled all the caskets and finally got to the last one, which the undertaker had fallen through. The doctor opened it and found the rich man's body with his arms and legs cut off and lying on top of his body. This was the only way the rich man would fit into the poor man's casket. In both of the rich man's hands were big pieces of skin that the hands had pulled off the undertaker's legs."

18. The Lucky Shot

"This was way back that winter that you couldn't barely find any wild animals to shoot," said Mack. "Well, one day when Charley was coming back from wasting all his shot on running game, he just had one piece left when he saw three turkeys sitting on a rail fence. Now Charley knew he could get one of them turkeys but he needed all three. So he was real quiet and crept close, and shot the rail and split it, and caught all three of them turkeys' toes in that crack. Now myself, I've killed two with one shot but never got three."

19. The Continual Liar

"A man came tearing along the road on his horse. Some men, stopping work in the field, said, 'Here's the biggest liar in the country. Let's stop him and hear him tell a few.'

"They asked him to tell them some lies.

" 'Tell lies nothing! This is no time to tell a lie. Your wife has just broke her leg, Tom, and I'm dashing to the doctor.'

"Tom rushed home, where he found his wife sweeping the yard."

20. The Land of the Lazy

"Just after the Civil War, at the beginning of the Reconstruction period in the South, some carpetbaggers came to Jackson County, Florida, in the hopes of making an easy living through the ignorance of the newly freed slaves.

"The carpetbaggers went to the numerous Negro shanties scattered throughout the farmlands of Jackson County and sold the colored people tickets to heaven.

"In this sales venture they told the Negroes that they would give them a ticket to heaven in exchange for what money or produce they might have, and the more they exchanged for the ticket the more elaborate wings, harps, and shrouds they would be given on a certain day (one day in the near future). Those with tickets were to meet St. Peter in Campbellton, Florida, a small community in the western part of Jackson County, and from there be led through the Golden Gates.

"The Negroes thought this was the most wonderful offer and gave more than they could spare of their meager belongings in exchange for a ticket.

"On the date set for the gathering in Campbellton it is said that the small community was black with colored people dressed in their best to meet St. Peter. They were wild with excitement, talking of their wings and wondering if they could play their harps.

"They waited way into the night for St. Peter, but it is said that he never did show up. So finally they gave up and went back to their homes.

"Also some carpetbaggers used a similar scheme and exchanged tickets for Africa, where the sweet taters grew as big as their heads, molasses ran out of the tree trunks, and watermelons were always ripe.

"The place where the Negroes were to meet the train for this trip was Cottondale, a small railroad crossing in the central part of Jackson County.

"On that day it is said that the Negroes came in the hundreds, and when the regular train did come into Cottondale they had to beat the colored people off with sticks as they were sure it was their train to Africa."

21. Larger than Life

"Well, I was a night watchman," said Mack. "I was a pretty good watchman, too. Never went to sleep much. But this night I was tired and kind of dozed off and got to dreaming about falling off the bridge into the water. That woke me up with a start, when I hit the water in my dream. Anyway, when I woke up, I found I had kicked my lantern off the bridge into the water. I looked down and could kind of see a faint glimmer, but I wasn't fixing to go down and retrieve it.

"Some five or six years later, I was fishing off that same bridge in about the same place where I kicked my lantern over. Well, I felt something heavy on my line when I went to bring it up. So I pulled and pulled and got it up, and I'll be damned if it wasn't that lantern still burning."

A neighbor named Martin was sitting nearby and couldn't let Mack's story go unchallenged. He said, "About a month ago

I went fishing down in the Gulf. We were about ten miles out when I set up my lines. Saw one of them kind of quiver, so I pulled it in, and on the hook was a beautiful ten-pound freshwater bass."

One of the onlookers who hadn't opened his mouth the whole time exclaimed, "You old fellows are getting too old to tell all those lies. Better be making peace with your Maker instead of making the devil smile."

To which Mack replied, "If he'll knock ten pounds off his fish, I'll blow out my lantern. . . ."

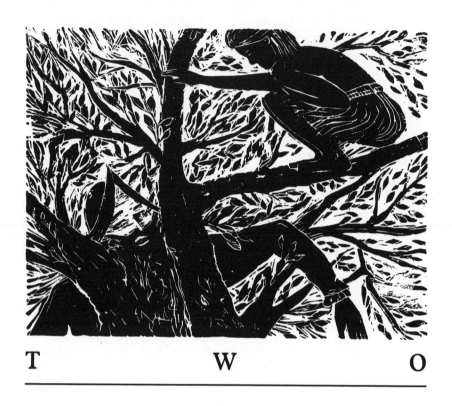

T   W   O

Legends

22. Origin of Seminole Clans and Black People

Variant A

"A long time ago when the Indians were emerging from a mountain, God spoke to the Panther clan and the Wind clan when they were still like ten-month-old babies. God told them to come out of the mountain. So they dug and dug and were the first of the forty-seven Seminole clans to come out. They were like brothers.

"Deer and Wolf clans were very close since they both had four feet. Then the Snake and all the other clans came out. The Snake clan was called king.

"Thus the Indians came out of the mountain first and last of all came the Negro. He stayed in the mud so long that when he emerged he was coal black."

Variant B

"Panther clan followed Wind clan from the navel of the earth. Panther had a big head and couldn't get out. The Wind clan came out like a whirlwind and came out on one side of tree roots which grew on a mound while Panther clan came out on the other side. Bird clan came out third and Snake last.

"The trees grew up so fast that Panther was held down at first. Wind clan blew up the roots and then Panther clan came out followed by Bird and Snake. They came out by the mound just like new babies. Just before they came from the navel of the earth they took a bath.

"Jesus said, 'I am coming back in twelve months.' He came back in ten months and that is how the clans were born."

23. The Flood

"A long time ago somebody made a houseboat and put all the animals in it. One man and one woman were there. Snake, Bear, Wolf, Deer, Buffalo—all of them. Indians were in the houseboat too.

"Then came the rain which lasted forty days and forty nights. Water was all around as far as the eye could see. After this it stopped raining and land was nowhere to be found. Pretty soon little birds with green sprigs in their mouths hove in sight. So the animals and the Indians knew there must be land somewhere even though they couldn't see it. They waited a little while, maybe a week, till the water went away and left them on top of a big hill."

24. The Giants of Florida

Variant A

"There is a large hammock up north of Lake Okeechobee where the tall men live. They are as tall as trees. Some of them stand up. Though they have bones like ordinary people, no living Indians have ever seen the giants. A long while ago there was a man, a very smart man, who went up to the cabbage woods and saw the giants. He told the rest of the people about them. These giants stand still all the time like a tree. Others lie down all the time like a log. They are dangerous and have the power to make a person sick.

"People go far off into the woods as if they were crazy when they have the giant sickness. They act as though something had hit them, but they have no idea what is the matter with them. They talk about seeing giants. If a person talks about looking at a giant, the medicine man knows what the trouble is."

Variant B

"Tate's Hell is a swamp on the other side of Carrabelle; it is very spooky-looking and the legend goes that no man that has ever gone in Tate's Hell has ever come out, that is except Mr. Tate himself. Tate was a fisherman from Carrabelle; he was big and strong and had long black curly hair, and he was more intelligent than most of the other fishermen around. Well, Tate heard about this swamp since he was a little boy, and so he decided to explore this massive swamp as soon as he became a man.

"He started out when he was in his early twenties. He entered the swamp all alone, doing it this way because he didn't want to be responsible for anyone else, and also because he didn't have too many volunteers to go with him. After he had been gone for several weeks, with nothing bothering him 'cept the gators, panthers, and snakes, and he wasn't really afraid of them 'cause he was used to them, he came to a huge clearing that sat high and dry and had green grass growing everywhere and one big oak sitting right in the middle of the clearing.

"Tate decided he would rest for a while, so he leaned against this big oak, and no sooner had he closed his eyes did he see this vision, or perhaps a dream. There standing right in front of him was this giant man; he just stood there looking at Tate, and Tate was just looking at him, too scared to do much of anything else. The only funny thing about this giant was that he was completely bald-headed.

"This giant motioned for Tate to follow him and they started off through the swamp, with Tate going as fast as he could to keep up with the giant's huge stride. After what seemed an eternity to Tate, they came to another clearing that was much larger and prettier than the other one. Here there were other giants and several giant women. Tate used to say he had never seen such beautiful women in all his life; they had long black hair and olive-white skin.

"It seems these giants took a liking to Tate, mostly because of his long curly black hair. Well, these giants liked him so much that they decided to give him one of their women. Well, Tate was deeply flattered, as any man would have been. After about two weeks of living in this paradise, Tate started to lose weight and his black hair started turning gray.

"One night he decided he best get out of there while he could because these giants were strange people, and besides, this woman was just too much for him, so he sneaked away and ran all the way back to Carrabelle. When he got to Carrabelle he didn't have a scratch on him and everyone was amazed. The only thing that had happened to him was that his beautiful black hair had turned completely white."

25. Origin of Spanish Moss

"After many long months at sea, Spanish sailors landed in Florida upon sighting some beautiful Indian maidens who were sunbathing on the beach. One Spaniard chased a beautiful maiden into the woods. But she trotted up a tree out of his reach.

"He was out of breath when he reached the tree, so he rested for a while. Then he climbed the tree after her. She moved up to the tip-top of the tree on a real small limb, and as he reached up to get her, he lost his balance and fell.

"His head was caught in the crotch of the tree. His body decayed, but his beard grew on and on . . . making the Spanish moss."

26. Origins of Seminole Indian Food

"Corn women lived in the woods and were big, fat, and heavy. Their bodies were made like a big ear of corn. They scraped their legs and kernels fell off on the ground.

"One time a corn woman stole a little Indian boy scarcely four weeks old. She took him home and fed him on corn kernels. He grew big and strong. When he was grown the corn woman returned him. He was soon married.

"Corn woman gave him four kernels of corn from which he grew four large plants. Soon the family had plenty of corn. When it was all gathered it filled a huge chest. That is the way the Indians obtained corn.

"Indians got pumpkin from Jesus at the same time they got koonti. Jesus had a pocketful of pumpkin seeds. The other pocket was full of turkey feathers. Jesus used to catch turkeys for the Indian boys."

27. Origin of Hushpuppies

"Ah wuz workin' hard all day an' when Ah wen' home Ah feels sick, mos' ready to die. Ah fell 'sleep at las'. Den de Lawd cum to me in my stakle [dream] and call me down to da edge o' de lake.

"When Ah gits dere Ah hear de Lawd say to me: 'Turn your bread aroun'!' Den He tell me how to make *p'noblums*.

"An' Ah been makin' um evah since. Ah paraded um all roun' da country. Ya cain' go nowheres without ya see p'noblums.

"Folks asks me why mah fish ain' got bones. They ain' fish. They's *p'noblums!*"

28. Origin of Packenham's Rum
(The Corpse in the Cask)

Along the Gulf Coast a particular kind of rum is called "Packenham." Helen Weaver of Tallahassee learned of its origin from her father:

"We hear a lot about General Jackson in this part of Florida around Tallahassee. Jackson was our commander at the Battle of New Orleans. The English commander was Packenham. My great-grandfather had a cousin, Henry Hunter, who was a soldier in that battle, and it is likely that he fired the shot that killed General Packenham.

"When my father was a boy of ten, old Henry was ninety and blind. He would sit for hours telling of fighting the Indians and hunting for bear and deer. As you know from your history books, General Jackson's men were made up of frontiersmen from Tennessee and Kentucky, men who were expert at shooting the long rifles. Henry Hunter was one of these men. His home was in west Tennessee.

"While the battle was raging, the English general could be seen walking back and forth on the breastworks waving a sword and urging his men on. With his red coat, white ruffled shirt front, and white trousers, he made a splendid target. Now I quote old Henry: 'My officer came to me and said, "Hunter, can you see the General?" "Of course," I said. "Do you think you could bring him down from there?" "Well," I said, "I've killed many a deer on Half Pone (a small mountain in west Tennessee) as far away as he is." "Well, load your gun heavy and take careful aim, and see if you can get him." I did load heavy and got a good bead on his chest. When I fired he fell. Of course, others were shooting, and I never could be sure, but I heard afterwards that there was a wound right where I held.'

"It was the general's express wish that should he be killed in battle his body should be sent to England for burial, for he did not want to lie dead in rebel soil. In those days sailors were superstitious about carrying a corpse on board, so the officer in charge smuggled the body on board the ship. As no embalming was done in those days, they drew out about two-thirds of the contents from a barrel of rum, removed the corpse's head [since the body was too long to fit in the barrel], placed the body of the general inside, and placed the head beside the body. After this odoriferous work was finished, the barrel was hidden deep in the hold of the ship sailing for England.

"The passage was long and rough. The weather was stormy, the grog was not plentiful, and food was limited. The unhappy sailors did a lot of complaining.

"Finally an old salt went prowling around down in the ship and found the barrel in which the general was hidden. He reported to his mates as to how the officers were holding out on the men and hiding a whole barrel of rum for their own use. Since the men were just as smart as any officer, they soon had a gimlet, bored a hole in the barrel, and drew out enough each day for a little nip all around—on the sly, of course.

"The poor old general was almost dry when he was opened up for the funeral. When the sailors found out what had happened, they were sorry they had been so eager to doubt the motives of their officers.

"Anyway, it is said that all around the Gulf Coast that particular kind of rum is called 'Packenham.' "

29. Early St. Augustine

E. L. Reyes recounted an episode from times when settlers and Indians lived closely together:

"Mr. E. T. Jencks, who owned a farm along North River as well as property in St. Augustine where the Marion Hotel now stands, needed food for the many workers on his farm. To help supply this food he was in the habit of stealing meat from the Indians. Finally the Indians sent word to him through an interpreter to warn him to stop robbing them; but he paid no attention to them. Since he wouldn't listen to their warning, the Indians started on the warpath against him.

"Probably getting advance word from one of his field workers, Jencks got scared and had the windows of his house barred.

"Then he sent out an interpreter to tell the Indians that he was in his basement sitting on a keg of powder. If they wanted to come get him, they could all be blown to hell. The Indians didn't come.

"Afterwards he fled to St. Augustine and took to the sea. Some say he became a St. Augustine pirate rivaling Gasparilla of Tampa."

Mrs. Reyes, descendent of the Llambias family headed by T. Llambias, member of the original Minorcan colony, liked the legends about the old St. Augustine cathedral, which was begun in 1793, some thirty years after her ancestor had constructed the two-story coquina building now known as the Llambias House:

"The beautiful silver chandelier in the old St. Augustine cathedral has connected with it a legend handed down through many generations of the oldest families. It is said that a seafaring man, being caught in a bad storm on the ocean, prayed for help and promised the Blessed Virgin that if he was saved he would make a lasting present to the first port of safety he entered. The cathedral chandelier represents the fulfillment of his promise.

"There are four bells in the old St. Augustine cathedral. One is in the extreme north by itself. This bell was called for many years the 'Agony Bell' during the old Spanish days. The name came from the custom of ringing this bell whenever a person was dying. When anyone heard it, he was to get on his knees and say a few prayers for the dying one. But when there was a very severe yellow fever epidemic in the 1880s (about '86 or '87), with many people dying, the bell was no longer rung. The Agony Bell has not been used since."

Mr. Reyes explained the public outcry around 1834 or 1835 against Sorrell Mead, a local engineer known familiarly as Red Top, who had been spending money on St. Augustine's fort, building a sea wall and damming up the waters. Construction had begun as early as 1672 on the quadrangular, moated fort, designed by Vauban, a French military engineer. St. Augustine had been defended by its wooden forts before city residents joined with soldiers, black slaves, and Indian hostages to erect the Castillo de San Marcos, a bastioned coquina fortress, completed in 1756. Known as Fort St. Marks under the British, changed to San Marcos under the Spanish, it became Fort Marion in 1825 when Florida became United States territory. Now, about ten years later, the fortress that had cost millions of dollars was being threatened. The handbill circulated to the populace called Red Top a "pretended engineer and real dunce" for pursuing his "waste and rascality." He was spending tens of thousands of dollars on stopping the free flow of the water that had drained through sluices into the ocean. His engineering had changed these waters around the fort so that they "must stagnate and stink like his own foul buzzard carcass." People were dying by the scores from the malaria that he had caused.

The people claimed that Mead had committed a "gross absurdity" in building a sea wall around the "old, worthless fort." A public meeting was called to make him stop his extravagance and his pestilence, as well to decide whether "sorrell Top shall be pickled like a *cabbage head;* or *shall be well Tarred, and his combustible Poll* ignited by a lucifer match, in full blaze, be cast like a New England witch, into the deep waters of the Matanzas." In the river he might be food for the "Herring Hogs," or if they turned up their noses at such "stinking meat," or if even the Devil refused to let him rot and be devoured, then the public would have him "boxed up in a *Tin Peddler's cart*" and "be carted beyond the limits of Florida—even to the Gallows— Thence to Hell! There forever to remain! For which God be praised!!! Amen. Amen. Laus Deo." Thus the residents of St. Augustine defended themselves against their own fort.

When the Civil War broke out, Mrs. Reyes said, an ancestor of hers was imprisoned in the Castillo de San Marcos:

"During the Civil War my aged grandfather Llambias, refusing to swear the oath of allegiance to the United States, was confined in the fort. Although his wife begged him to give in to the northerners' request, he said, 'You wouldn't, and I won't either.'

"But, you know, there is always some good person in any group to help you. A Yankee general ordered him released. He fled with his family from the northern-occupied city to Tallahassee. His wife took nothing but her silver with her. They walked by day and slept on cots they managed to carry along. Grandfather Llambias died in Tallahassee and is buried there.

"When the rest of the family returned to St. Augustine after the war, all they found left in the house was one big table. The floor boards had been cut out and pigs kept in the house."

In a lighter vein Mr. Reyes reminisced about an old St. Augustine character:

"In St. Augustine there once lived a man with very short legs. They weren't particularly noticeable while he was sitting, but when he stood it looked as though he had fallen up to his torso through a hole in the floor. The story has it that whenever his wife had trouble with him she lifted him up onto the mantelpiece, where he was forced to stay until he promised to behave."

30. *José Gaspar*

Alice Welch knew the fullest version of this famous pirate's life. According to her, José was born in Barcelona in 1756. When he was eighteen years old, he entered the Barcelona Naval Academy, where he received his appointment as a lieutenant in the Spanish Navy. At this point the historical records vanish and, as Alice said, "legend takes over."

"There are various accounts of just how José Gaspar first turned to piracy. The first and probably most logical of these is that Gaspar, fighting in the war against England, was on board the *Florida Blanca* when it was forced to put farther out to sea for safety. He and the other young cadets became increasingly more restless for adventure and plotted together to mutiny and seize the ship; Gaspar's boon companion and accomplice was Roderigo Lopez. After the successful and bloody mutiny Gaspar and his companions headed for the West Indies and Florida to find adventure and treasures. It was during this trip that he changed his name to the more mellifluous one of Gasparilla, and also, in order to disguise the *Florida Blanca*, rechristened it the *Gasparilla I*.

"Another version relates that while Gaspar was a student at the Spanish Naval Academy he became quite a favorite at the court, and especially so with the ladies. He found an opportunity and attempted to steal the crown jewels, but was detected in the act, fled, seized the ship *Florida Blanca*, and turned pirate.

"Still another is that Gaspar, while on land duty, conceived the idea of leaving the country in a stolen ship and turning pirate. This he did, leaving behind a wife and two children.

"Sailing around the coast of Florida he discovered Charlotte Harbor with its four small islands just inside the mouth. He made his headquarters on the northernmost one, which he named Gasparilla Island. The others were named Pine Island, for the dense growth found there; Sanibel, at the request of Roderigo Lopez, whose Spanish sweetheart was of that name; and Captiva, because it was here that he kept his prisoners. It was on Captiva, so the legend goes, that the buccaneer kept his harem, but no fragile bones or bits of jewelry have ever been discovered. However, Gasparilla is said to have beheaded a Spanish princess, one of his captives, when she refused his love. She was buried on the island, and there are those who swear that when a grave was discovered and opened the female skeleton was found with the skull sliced off.

"Gasparilla himself always claimed that he offered women captives as wives to those of his men who might choose them, insisting on a form of marriage ceremony, performed by a padre whom he had taken captive off one of his plundered ships, and enforcing strict respect of the marital relation by other pirates.

"There is a story that Gasparilla was engaged to a beautiful girl in Barcelona and planned to marry her as soon as peace came and he could obtain shore leave. However, his love for the sea was too great and, although he often talked about her to the other pirates and wrote of her in his diary, he never returned to claim her. She, in turn, thinking he had been lost at sea during a storm, married another and supposedly lived happily ever after.

"Nevertheless, when Ann Jeffrey, an English lady, became his captive he is said to have fallen very much in love with her and courted her in a gentlemanly fashion. She would not return his love, however, and at length told him she was in love with another, a certain Batista Fuentes. Gasparilla, although angered at first and plotting to kill them both, put them on a ship, which he plundered, ordered a marriage ceremony to be performed as soon as the ship was out of his sight, and sent them off to England.

"Suddenly one day a strange ship came into the range of the lookout, and, changing its course, headed directly toward Gasparilla's lair. When it was close enough to see with the naked eye, the band on shore saw the pirate flag flying from her mast; soon a boat was lowered over the side, loaded with men, and put off for the pier. When they landed, the tall, handsome leader introduced himself as Jean Lafitte, the French buccaneer who plundered the waters around New Orleans, and said he had come to pay a social visit and get acquainted with his fellow pirates. Several weeks later, Gasparilla, Lafitte, and their men captured a British slave-trader, loaded on a run from Africa to New Orleans. Gasparilla was only interested in cargoes of jewels, gold, or rum, but Lafitte offered to take the valuable human cargo to New Orleans, sell it, and return one-half of his profits to Gasparilla. So Lafitte and his men sailed away with the African slaves, but never returned to bring Gasparilla his share.

"Roderigo Lopez, still Gasparilla's closest companion, was becoming homesick for Spain, and after a new ship was captured, he asked José's permission to take the old ship and a crew of men who would be willing, and sail for Spain. Gasparilla agreed, and they left, not to be heard of for eight years. Eight years later, however, the pirate band seized a British square-rigger, and on board was Roderigo Lopez. The old *Gasparilla I* had been lost in a storm on the way back to Spain, and the few who escaped in a lifeboat were picked up by a merchant vessel going to Liverpool. From there Roderigo made his way to Barcelona, where he married his Sanibel, and told the story that the *Florida Blanca* had been lost in a wreck on the Florida coast, and José Gasper with it. However, when he returned to Spain Roderigo had taken Gasparilla's diary as a memento of his chief and had given it to Sanibel for safekeeping. In it were recorded all of the activities and exploits of the pirate band and particulars of the raided ships. She let it fall into the hands of the Spanish authorities, and they in turn asked help of the United States in capturing this infamous pirate. It is from this diary that some of the stories of Gasparilla originate.

"Legends say that Gasparilla accumulated some thirty million dollars in loot, which he buried somewhere on Gasparilla Key. After forty years of pirating, late in 1821, Gasparilla decided to retire to South America and live peaceably for the remainder of his days. The entire band was gathered together for the purpose of dividing the pirate loot that had been accumulated when a strange, promising-looking ship appeared on the horizon. It gave the appearance of a wealthy merchant ship with valuable cargo, and possibly rich passengers aboard. This was more than any of them could stand; so they decided to make one last plunder.

"They boarded the *Gasparilla II* and hurried out to encounter the vessel. As they did, the British flag that the other ship had been flying slipped down, and in its place was raised the American flag; the canvas disguises fell from the guns, and the ship was revealed as the *U.S. Enterprise*, on the search for pirates. They immediately opened fire on the *Gasparilla II*, and within a few minutes the ship was sinking. Gasparilla, realizing that there was no way of escape, wrapped himself in his anchor chain and jumped overboard, flashing his sword over his head. This was the end of Gasparilla, the last of the buccaneers, according to legend, but the U.S. Navy has no record of any such capture; in fact, at the time of the supposed seizure the records show that the *Enterprise* was at a point far from that of the Gasparilla lair.

"To this day the buried treasure of Gasparilla has not been discovered, although many optimists have been, and still are, searching for it. And in the spring of every year the city of Tampa surrenders, for a week of merrymaking, to a mock invasion by Gasparilla and his mystic crew."

31. The Dark Nights in May

"The Spanish galleon lurched in the tropical bay like a wounded swan. In the glow of sunset the pirate ship like a vulture slid alongside. A wave of yellow, disheveled men, reeking and filthy, poured above to continue the fight. The crew on the galleon fought bitterly until all were strewn like crumpled bits of paper over the decks and hold.

"The pirates, eager for loot, swarmed down the gangway. Captain Gaspar, striding ahead, reached the closed stateroom door first and kicked it open.

"Surprise stopped him in his tracks. As the men peered over his shoulder into the twilight gloom of the cabin, silence spread, until only the lapping of the water was heard.

"There before them was a señora, her pale beauty seeming to light the room. In the face of death, she stood with the bearing of a princess. Her white lace mantilla fell over her blue-black hair in a cascade.

"Gaspar on a sudden impulse broke the silence with a bellow, saying the first man to touch her would die by his hand.

"The men collapsed in heaps on the deck of the ship. In amazement they looked at the notorious Gaspar, Terror of the Gulf, courteously leading the señora to the deck and placing her violin in her arms.

"With a sweeping bow, Gaspar backed to the rail and jumped over to the waiting boat.

"The order to set sail rang clear. Gaspar stood in the stern of the receding vessel and watched the outline of a white mantilla in the blackening night.

"Long-drawn tones of the violin stole over the water, beginning the never-ending melody that can still be heard in the dark nights of May."

32. The She-Man

"As the story goes, there was once a strange hermit who resided in the swamplands of the Caloosahatchee. He wore a dress and lived off the fish and wildlife of the swamplands. He was a ragged and dirty old man who disliked people and was of a nature that made him withdraw from civilization completely. Many people on hunting expeditions had seen the man around his native haunts hunting and fishing, but had never approached him because of the belief that he was insane.

"The 'She-Man,' as he was known to citizens, was a fearful sight to those hunters who by accident stumbled into the woods where he did his hunting. Often hunters would run away in fright after seeing this weird creature in the woods.

"Once a man reported that while hunting one day he noticed an eight-foot alligator splashing along the banks of one of the shallow marshes. When he started to take aim on the creature with his rifle, he noticed that the alligator was following a dirty, bearded man. The man was wearing a woman's skirt and walking toward the banks of the creek. The hunter hesitated to fire on the alligator for fear of hitting the man, but upon further observation he realized that the alligator was a pet of the bedraggled creature it was following. Not knowing whether or not the man was insane, the hunter returned to the 'less wild' part of the swamp.

"Rumors about the old man have flourished for many years. The more consistent ones relate that he went crazy as the result of his wife's death. Ever since this happened, he has worn her clothes and lived apart from the rest of the civilized world.

"Before his wife's death, when the 'She-Man' was living in a little one-room log hut near the Caloosahatchee River with his wife and son, he had gotten into an argument with the landlord, Mr. Morgan, for whom he was working. Mr. Morgan was a direct descendent of the famous pirate Morgan. Many people in that area believed that when he died the old pirate had left his stolen fortune in the hands of Mr. Morgan. Morgan ordered the 'She-Man' off his land after the brawl and pitched him out of house and home. The 'She-Man' had no money, so he took to the swamps with his family to make their home in the woods.

"From the few tools he had been able to keep, he improvised a little lean-to in which they lived for a number of years. He fashioned a bed out of raw cotton, a chair out of gourds, and his fire burned on a flat stone. Near his handmade home he kept his pet alligator named Devil, who obeyed his master like a dog.

"Some years after he moved into the wilds of the jungle he came face to face with Morgan while on one of his hunts for food. Morgan had secretly rowed up the river in search of a safe place to bury a chest of gold from his pirate uncle's treasure, when he accidentally bumped into the 'She-Man.' Being unaware of what Morgan had in the trunk that lay in the rear of the boat, the 'She-Man' indifferently engaged Morgan in conversation. After Morgan's attempts to be friendly had somewhat smoothed the differences between the two men, the 'She-Man' invited Morgan to have supper with him. Morgan accepted eagerly, and the two strolled back toward the wild man's home.

"After the supper of fish and corn fritters, Morgan asked the 'She-Man's' son Jim if he would accompany him on a fishing trip that night. The young boy accepted willingly.

"When the two did not return by the midnight hour, the father and mother began to worry about their son. They decided that they had better go in search of the two in case something had happened to them; so the father set out toward the east and the mother toward the north in their search. When the father had searched unsuccessfully for hours, he decided that he had better return home.

"Upon arriving back at the camp, he found no one there. The mother had not returned, and neither had the boy and Morgan, so he set out at a hurried pace in the direction his wife had taken. About two miles from the camp, he began to get frantic as he ran along the narrow path. All of a sudden he stumbled over a body lying crumpled in the path. Reaching down, he felt his wife's limp body lying in a heap. Her body was still warm, and her breath came in faint gasps as he tried to revive her. She had run some distance before tripping on a root and hitting her head on a cypress knee. He noticed that a long gash on the side of her head had been bleeding and had matted her hair in dark red clots. She regained consciousness long enough to tell her husband what had happened; then she died.

"Morgan and Jim had been down the river beside a deep pit, which the two had dug when she came up on them. She noticed that Jim had placed the trunk in the pit and was filling in dirt beside it when Morgan slipped around behind him and stabbed him in the back three times. Jim's body fell over the trunk and Morgan finished filling the pit, covering the boy's body with the trunk.

"When she told of this, she fainted dead away and died shortly thereafter. The 'She-Man' set out in search of Morgan as soon as he saw that his wife was dead. His pet alligator, Devil, was close on his heels as he ran madly in search of Morgan.

"Nearly an hour later he saw Morgan's raft in the middle of the river and dived into the water after him. When he reached the raft, he capsized it and yelled for Devil to get him. The alligator slid hungrily into the water after his prey. In nearly a minute's time Devil was seen churning the water around where Morgan went down and a dark reddish-black substance colored the moonlit water of the Caloosahatchee. Then, all was quiet save the smacking sounds coming from the jaws of Devil as he enjoyed his meal. From this time on, the man that Morgan had once kicked out of house and home roamed the woods wearing his wife's clothes, with a dazed, far-off look in his eyes. His beard grew longer and matted with mud, his clothes hung in shreds, and his appearance grew more and more like that of a wild man, out of touch with the civilized world about him. After that day he was known to the people in that area as the 'She-Man' of the Caloosahatchee.

"Not many years after the death of his wife, he vanished. Whether he died or not is not known. No bones were ever found near his home, and no one has ever found the treasure that Morgan buried near the river that night. Wherever it is—if it is still there—there will be found lying under the trunk a boy's skeleton. And in the trunk is believed to be all that remains of the once bodacious and reckless pirate Morgan who looted and plundered Spanish gold all along the Florida coast many years ago."

33. *Choosing the Site for the State Capitol*

"A group of citizens from the principal towns in territorial Florida assembled in St. Augustine for the purpose of selecting a place for the State Capitol. After much deliberation and many controversies and disputes regarding the central location for this building, it was agreed by those present that the two most able horsemen in the territory, one from the east and one from the west, would be the deciding factors in the solving of the problem.

"The horsemen's itineraries were complete in every intricate detail. They were to mount their horses at a specified time on a certain day; they were to ride from sunup to sundown at the same rate of speed, stop for rest at designated intervals, and the spot where they met would be the site of the Government House.

"It is said that they met approximately three miles south of Tallahassee in the lowland. They then rode their horses over the hills and a stake was driven where the Capitol now stands.

"When the Honorable Richard Call was chosen as Territorial Governor in this northern region, he took his oath of office in the small, crude, unpretentious building that was built on the spot where the horsemen planted the stake."

34. Legendary Tallahassee

a. Aunt Memory

"There was the old slave, Aunt Memory. Her story is one that all Tallahassee people know because she was a mixture of old superstitions and her life portrays the ways of her race. She rose to have her own property and social standing. She worked for the Demilly family and would never work for anyone else. She had an old boyfriend known as Uncle Tom who built her a home on College Avenue, and she could be seen sweeping all the pathway leading up to her house because she felt that any disturbance in the ground was the work of someone who wanted to conjure her. She always carried her broom with her so that wherever she walked she was sure that her broom would get rid of anything that wanted to harm her. She carried a clock, an umbrella, and a satchel in addition to her broom and could always be recognized because she carried these four things with her. She had her own well in the house and would never let anyone get near it because that too would be an easy way for someone to conjure her. Aunt Memory also had a flying jenny of her very own and would sit by it and work away. She insisted on getting her pay in silver and each night would sit down and polish all her silver coins.

"Old Aunt Memory was the only Negro from Tallahassee to visit the Chicago Exposition of the 1890s. She started off on the train carrying along her coffeepot and some kindling because she thought that the train would stop and let her fix a cup of coffee. After she reached Chicago she was really treated royally and welcomed by some of her friends. She always claimed that she came from Virginia although no one knows how she ever got here to begin with. After she returned she would say to everyone she saw who went to the fair, 'Did you see me? I was there and I was important, too!'—this to the delight of everyone who heard her. She really believed that she was important."

b. Tiger Tail

"There is an old legendary hero known as Tiger Tail who was an Indian chief of a tribe of Indians that was always friendly with the white settlers. The old Demilly family knew Tiger Tail, as Mr. Demilly was a trader with the Indians. The children used to pass along the Indian territory to get to their schoolhouse and Tiger Tail said that at times he would be within distance to reach out and touch them, but they were never bothered. Such was the friendship of that Indian tribe."

c. The Osceola Oak Tree

"A story is told about a tree on the Lafayette land grant. This tree was called the Osceola Oak and was located near the Carraway place between the Carraways and the highway, about two hundred yards from the highway. The story is that Osceola's father was a white man named Powell and his mother was a Creek Indian. Powell decided to build a house on this site and after it was built he welcomed those men who brought whiskey and other things to trade with the Indians. During the night he would take their money and kill these traders. In this way Powell managed to make his living. He was a very cruel man and especially mean to the Indians so that after his death they wanted to get rid of everything that would remind them at all of Powell. That is why they tried to deaden the oak that was in front of the house, but, try as they would, the tree seemed to be protected against all their efforts because it would never die."

d. Lake Legends

"There are many legends about the lakes around Tallahassee, particularly because of the fact that they will appear and become as big as twelve miles wide and will then recede to a point of dryness that makes it possible for a car to drive right where the lakes were. An old Tallahassee resident, Mr. Whitfield, said that he had driven along where the bottom of Lake Jackson is now.

"An old man in town used to say that there was no bottom at all to Lake Mystic, and although people do swim across it, no one has touched the bottom of the lake."

d1. Lake Ella

"As late as 1925 the people in Tallahassee said that the lake known as Lake Ella had no real name. At one time a man named Mr. Bull was courting a girl named Ella and they would go down and sit at the edge of this lake. They were really sweet on each other and Mr. Bull wanted to marry Ella. The night that he proposed there by the lake he said that for her, then and there, he would call this 'sheet of water' Lake Ella. Before they were married, though, Ella told him that she had changed her mind; so Mr. Bull went back to the place and said that from then on the lake would be known as Bull Pond, not Lake Ella. Some of the oldest settlers are still true to his memory and refer to Lake Ella as Bull Pond."

d2. Lake Jackson

"At one time there was a young Indian girl who fell in love with a brave who had been ostracized by their tribe. He had betrayed the faith of the Indians in this tribe by siding with the white men when they came. The couple realized that their love could never be recognized by their friends and so they asked their gods for help. One day, in the face of some of those who knew them, they joined hands, and where they had been standing there suddenly came forth a very clear spring and the two lovers vanished. The water from this spring was gradually centered and is now known as Lake Jackson."

d3. Lake Miccosukee

"When Andrew Jackson came to Florida he found a very fierce tribe of Indians who were led by Chief Miccosukee. When Jackson learned of their activities he discovered that they had three hundred white men's scalps in their possession. After he conquered these Indians he decided that he would leave a mark for all to see and know that he was the conqueror, so he wrote on a stone, 'A. Jackson.' Today this stone is at the bottom of what is known as Lake Miccosukee and can be seen when the water recedes."

e. The Cherokee Rose

"There was a young Seminole Indian brave who was fighting with his tribe when he met and fell in love with a Cherokee Indian maiden. She decided to go with him. Before she left her people, though, those who loved her knew that she was leaving all that she had grown up with, and to keep their memory with her, they gave her a rose bush to take along to the new land in which she would be living. And so to the Seminole Indians there came a new flower, the rose, which they called after the girl's tribe, the Cherokees. Even today that rose is in Florida together with other species which have come down from the Carolinas."

f. Spanish Treasure

"A certain group of Spaniards came to Tallahassee and had a lot of pirate treasure that it was necessary to get rid of at the time. This was in the year 1845. They decided to build a house and, in each brick, place a piece of that silver which they had captured. They planned to return and retrieve the silver but never got back. This house is still standing and is known as the Columns." In recent years the house was moved to a new location to become the headquarters for the Tallahassee Chamber of Commerce.

g. The Goodwood Plantation

"The original owners of Goodwood Plantation decided to go on a sea voyage, but while they were gone they both died in a shipwreck. Both sides of the family contested for the property and no lawyers knew what to do about the case because there was no way to know which one had died first. They litigated and litigated and finally decided that it was a recognized fact that men were stronger than women and therefore the man had lived longer. The male side of the family received the property and were considered legal heirs."

h. The Smoky Swamp

"Around the 1880s there were many stories in Tallahassee about the smoke that would appear in the direction of Wakulla. The region in which the smoke appeared was an impenetrable swamp known as Gum Swamp. The foliage was of fern patches as big as trees, and cat claw briars. Some thought that a tribe of Indians were living back there, others believed that a hermit had somehow managed to get back into the solitude of the swamp, others believed that moonshiners were back in there making shiny. A New York newspaper sent two reporters down to see what they could find out. One of them lost his life in the search. After the Charleston earthquake in 1886 people began to notice that the swamp was becoming more and more passable. They were very anxious to get in there and find out what was causing the smoke, but much to their surprise the smoke suddenly disappeared.

"One afternoon many years later, Mrs. Cash, a Tallahassee resident, was standing on the front porch of the Wooten home in Waukeenah. As she looked in the direction of the Wacissa

Swamp she noticed some black smoke rising. She said that the smoke was the same color as the smoke that can be seen at cane grindings. The Negroes use a wood called lightwood in the furnaces that boil down the syrup. They use this wood because it is just the right size. Right away she asked the Wootens about it and they said that the smoke didn't appear every day, although it was seen quite often. They said that when it did come into sight it was in the afternoon between one and two o'clock. When Mr. Cash heard this, he said that it was caused by the same thing that causes such black smoke in Ireland, the Ireland peat bogs. The land around the peatwood dries out and this dry vegetation catches on fire and when it reaches the damp peatwood the peatwood won't burn but will smoke. What do you think?"

i. Prince Murat

"The most important legendary hero around these parts is Prince Murat, buried in a cemetery right in Tallahassee. Prince Murat was the nephew of Napoleon the Great and his wife was the grandniece of George Washington. His mother sent him money from France to live on when she was not spending it on one of her lovers.

"One time this Prince had a dinner party and invited some of his friends who were from the northern "civilized" parts of the United States. They were served what seemed to be the main course. After the meal they were mentioning that delicious meat and asked what in the world it was; whereupon they learned that they had been served buzzard. This same prince had a buzzard one night for dinner but found that it was entirely too tough to eat; so he buried it in the ground for about four days, then went out and dug it up and had quite an enjoyable repast.

"Prince Murat was a great experimenter along every line. One time he thought he had completely perfected a red dye. He took all of his wife's clothes and dyed them red.

"It is also said that Prince Murat was not so much on dressing himself up. As a matter of fact he was very careless and would wear clothes until they were so dirty that they would stick to him.

"There are many more stories about this legendary hero who, in the search for the rainbow's end and the ideal happiness, failed to make any money of his own and, though a prince, died a poor man."

j. Mrs. Lewis Lively

"At one time there were some falls down by the place where the Tallahassee railroad station is today. People called these falls the cascades and it is said that they were very beautiful, and the spot was one of the reasons why Tallahassee was chosen as the capital site. Everyone enjoyed the beauty until the year 1880, when a Mrs. Lewis Lively walked into the cascades and died. The people of Tallahassee were so alarmed they decided to fill up the place so that no one else would die in this way, since drowning was a very bad way to die. After hauling a lot of dirt they managed to stop the falls but they were not able to stop up the source of the cascades. The water is still running under the city of Tallahassee and is known as the Old St. Augustine Branch."

k. The Lafayette Tree

"For years and years the story was told in hushed tones about the old tree on the Lafayette land grant. The house near the tree had been abandoned and seemed almost 'hainted,' particularly with the added eerie effect of this old oak tree. On certain nights ghosts were seen all around the tree and no one could imagine why they should come to that special tree. Everyone was afraid to go near the tree, especially at night.

"Then one day there was a terrible thunderstorm and a bolt of lightning struck that tree. In the middle of the tree was found a very distinguishable human skeleton."

l. Old Man Eppes

"On the plantations in Tallahassee the Negroes used to have their own big parties at the end of a busy week. The white folks usually let them enjoy themselves privately, but one night Old Man Eppes decided to join them, for he was very much attracted to a young Negro slave. At the party he paid close attention to the young girl, much to the annoyance of a young man who was in love with her. As the evening went on and they drank more and more shiny, things got rougher and rougher and ended up in a fight in which Old Man Eppes was killed. The Negroes put him in a carriage and took him up to the plantation home, and thus he was found . . . dead. Until this day those who are near the house at night say that on nights when the moon is brightest they can hear the chanting of Negro voices and sometimes see the same old carriage coming up the pathway."

m. The White Goat

"One night a man came running out of old Gum Swamp and declared to everyone around that he had seen a big white goat. Now there was a young man who didn't believe this story and, if he did, wasn't frightened by it and determined to go on with one of his regular hunting trips. He hadn't gone very far into the swamp when he heard a rustling in the bushes. He rushed to the sound and there he saw directly in front of him a white ghostly-looking goat. He ran out of the woods as fast as he could. People haven't seen the goat in a long time, but there are some who still believe that it's there."

n. The Soft-Shelled Turtle

"One day an old Negro woman was walking along on the Biddle plantation and right beside her there was a kind of bank. She saw one of those big long-necked soft-shelled turtles at the top of the embankment and as she looked it started to roll down towards the path where she was. As she stood there and looked, it rolled and rolled and rolled and each time that it did roll it got smaller and smaller until it was a very small turtle. She kept watching and almost before she knew what was happening that turtle got littler and littler and finally vanished out of sight."

o. The Lop-Eared Dog

"One Sunday noon after church a Negress and her husband were walking home when they noticed a little dog trotting along between them. As they walked along, the dog stayed at their heels and finally began to get ahead of them. The farther it walked the larger it became, until it was the size of a big dog. There was only one thing that was peculiar about that dog. On one side the ear remained little, while the ear on the other side of the dog became big and lopped over like the ear of a cow."

p. The Vision

"Along the edge of the Biddle plantation there was a row of bushes, and among these bushes there was an oak tree. A little farther on there was a cherry tree. As two of the plantation Negro women were walking along to go to a pond to do their washing, there suddenly appeared by the oak tree another Negro wearing a white headdress and a white apron. She stood there for a while and remained still until they could see her fairly well. Then, instead of walking towards them, she walked backwards, and just as she reached the cherry tree she vanished out of sight. They never saw any more traces of her anywhere else, but then they never went back that particular way again."

q. Night Watch

"In the 1900s when people died there were no undertakers. The bodies would be washed and dressed and placed on a plank or some kind of props, and folks would take turns sitting up with the corpse. On one such instance there was a man sitting in a house in Tallahassee, and this man had the reputation of being a very honest citizen. As he sat there the door blew open. He got up and closed it and it blew open again. Just to make sure he wouldn't have to get up a third time, he bolted the door and returned to his watch. He had only been away from the door for a moment when it was blown open again, in spite of the strong bolt."

r. A Snake Attack

"One day the son of a Negro who was working on the Biddle plantation was out in the woods picking berries. He happened to notice a huge rattlesnake all coiled up and ready to strike. Now this scared the young boy so much that he wasn't able to make a sound. However, just at that moment a friend of his mother's happened along and saw the snake and the boy. Right away she yelled for the boy's mother and at the same time reached down to pick up a large stick that was nearby. With a powerful blow she hit that snake just as the boy's mother came along. As they examined the snake more closely they saw that he was about eight inches in diameter and, as nearly as they could figure out from the rattles, he had lived about twenty-nine years. But that wasn't the end of the experience. The woman had hit the snake right in the middle of his body and he had died. Right after this his mouth opened and about twenty-six little rattlesnakes came running out of it."

s. The St. Marks Cow

"Between St. Marks and Tallahassee there used to be many country homes where the people went to get away from the 'city life' of Tallahassee. As time went by, this land was broken up and small farmers moved in.

"To give an example of what the land was like there is the remembrance of a Florida State College for Women instructor. Just about fifteen or twenty years ago this teacher went down there digging for Indian relics, which she heard were buried around. There were two people with her, and they were all digging when suddenly the ground gave way and the teacher was buried in all that loose dirt.

"These small farmers had no idea what the land was like underneath and one of them, in order to have water on his place, decided to dig a well somewhere near his house. Now this particular farmer had a cow who stood by him as he worked daily, digging that well deeper and deeper. One morning the farmer was getting ready to dig and he thought that this would be the day he would strike water. When he went outside, though, the first thing he noticed was that his cow wasn't in sight. He immediately thought that the cow had wandered off someplace; then he heard a noise from the well that sounded just like it might be the cow but there was no way he could get to it.

"About two weeks later this farmer was down in St. Marks. To his astonishment he saw the cow, his very own cow that had fallen in the well. Evidently the cow had fallen in a cavern and found its way out near St. Marks."

t. Rain

"In any place where there is much rain, stories or good-natured slams will be told about it. On a rainy day here in Tallahassee I heard this story.

"One time a very bad storm was coming up and it looked like once the rain started it would never stop. A farmer looked up and saw the sky and immediately called his hired man in. He told him that they were really going to profit by the rain this time. The farmer told the hired man that the cow they had butchered the last fall was in their deep freeze. 'What I want you to do,' the farmer said, 'is to get those two sides of beef and put a little chunk of it on each of the barbs on our barbed-wire fence. From what I counted as we put up the fence, you will find 900,000 barbs out here, so you had better get to work right now.'

"Well, that hired man went and got the beef and started his

job and just finished it before the storm broke. He came rushing back to the farm house and he and the farmer sat together and watched the rain come down. It rained for days and days and finally the land could absorb no more water, so it started flooding. The water rose higher and higher and finally their whole farming area was flooded, and the barbed-wire fence was completely covered. The hired man still couldn't figure out why he had put the beef out there. Well, in due course of time the water receded and as it did so, it was possible to see that on each barb on the fence there was a fish. They ran out and started bringing in the fish and when they finished the farmer started counting them. Then, in a rage, he fired the hired man. You see, there were 900,000 barbs and they had just caught 899,999 fish."

u. Cows on the Road

"There was quite an interesting boy who lived here in Tallahassee, and around his life there have been many jokes and stories.

"Charles was, among other things, very nearsighted. One night a whole group of people were being driven down the highway with Charles behind the wheel. They all noticed some cows in the road ahead, but instead of slowing down to avoid them, Charles seemed to be heading right toward them. One of the boys yelled, 'Hey, Charles, watch out! There are cows in the road!' Charles answered, 'Cows in the road? Why, I thought those were specks on the windshield.' "

v. The Tallahassee Train

"The Tallahassee-Jacksonville train was never on time going in either direction. This was a fact sadly recognized by all those who resigned themselves, of necessity, to traveling on it. However, there was one day when the train pulled into Jacksonville just exactly on time. Everyone was overjoyed. To show appreciation to the engineer, some of the group decided that they would collect money from all the passengers. After getting together a considerable sum, the committee rushed up to the engineer and congratulated him. For a moment the man just gaped, then he looked around and said, 'Folks, I thank you, but there's something you ought to know. This here is yesterday's train.' "

35. Lost at Sea

"Some years ago a young Tallahassee couple were married here and left for Europe on their honeymoon. But the ship and its passengers were never seen again. Since each of the newlyweds was very wealthy and there was a large estate involved, complicated court proceedings were begun to see which family would get the money. The whole question was dependent upon which of the couple had lived longer. The court finally decided that since a man is stronger than a woman, he would be able to keep afloat longer. Therefore, since the bride had died first, her estate would go to the groom, and then at his death the joint estate would go to his family, the Brooms. So much hard feeling arose between the families that two monuments were erected to the memory of the young Broom couple to try to heal the break.

"This story is supposed to be absolutely true. I have heard from many Tallahasseeans minor variations of the same story."

36. Tallahassee Houses

In a city of considerable size, like Tallahassee, legends accumulate around family homes that have stirred people's imaginations through the years, sometimes because of peculiarities in the structure itself, at other times because of the sorts of people who lived in them. Newell Martin shared these legends with me during 1949:

"The Flagg house [323 East Park Avenue] was built of material taken from the first Capitol when it was taken down to be replaced by the new building in 1840. The windows were also the ones used in the first Capitol. The house was built by Capt. R. A. Shine.

"One of the stories told of this house was that one night Mr. Flagg and Mr. Dick Wilson were returning from playing cards with Capt. Pat Houston. As they passed this house Mr. Flagg told Mr. Wilson that he held a ticket for the Louisiana Lottery, due the next day, and if his was the lucky number he was going to buy that house, for the ticket was for the exact amount of money that was being asked for the house. The next day he was notified that his number was the chosen one, and that day the house became the Flagg home.

"Another tradition has it that one day, as a blind man was

sitting in one of the bay windows on the east side of the house, a bolt of lightning came from a clear sky and struck the outside window. The man was stunned, but when he recovered from the shock his sight had been restored.

"The Columns [102 South Adams Street (moved to 100 N. Duval)] house is one of the oldest buildings in Tallahassee. It is characterized by four round columns, its great size, and its huge chimneys that rise with the gable ends. The bricks are of a dark red color, and there is a legend that a nickel (or, some say, a penny) is molded in every brick.

"When you enter the front door you see at the back of the hall the stair with the Dominican mahogany rail leading to the floor above. This stair was not always as it is today, for—so the story goes—when the house was built the owner had the stairway run down through his bedroom on the first floor for fear his beautiful and rich young daughter would elope with someone who loved her only for her money.

"The DeMilly house [629 West Jefferson Street] was the first home of Mr. and Mrs. John L. DeMilly. Tradition says that the Indians lurked around this home so often that blankets had to be hung at the windows after it was found that blinds did not keep the Indians from peeping in.

"In the early days no one ventured to take the long, lonely path down the hill to town after night, and even in the daytime one would be lucky if he did not hear, or feel, an Indian creeping after him as he walked through the woods to his neighbors' house.

"Tallahassee and other sections of Florida are well noted for their beautiful japonica trees. The Thomas Holmes Hagner house [301 East Park Avenue] is connected with the coming of these trees to Florida.

"Katherine Gamble came to Tallahassee as the bride of Thomas Holmes Hagner, who was the U.S. Minister to the court of King George. The gardens around their home took in half the block. Beautiful azaleas, oleanders, camellias, crape myrtles, and rose bushes grew there. Legend tells us that here the japonica tree was first planted in Florida.

"In the hothouse of Katherine Gamble Hagner's Virginia home were many tubs of japonicas brought from the court of King George by General Messer as a gift to her mother. When the bride left for her new home in the sunny South, she brought with her these rare plants. They thrived and multiplied so well in her garden here that soon in all the Tallahassee gardens were small japonicas from these old bushes."

37. The Last Tallahassee Indians

Newell Martin told me how the last Indian left the Tallahassee region:

"For years people in Tallahassee had thought that all the Indians had at last gone either to South Florida or out West. From time to time, they still missed a few chickens or the like. They were convinced that perhaps a few Indians were returning to Tallahassee to steal at night.

"We are told that one day John McCall and his young son started out on a three-day trip to some point on the west coast of Florida. Mr. McCall was to see someone about a business deal, and little Johnny had persuaded him to let him go along.

"The first night they found a deserted cabin in which to spend the night. They fixed their beds in the loft and had just turned in for the night when they heard the door creak open. Two Indians had entered and were starting to build a fire in the old fireplace. Before they had finished, ten other Indians appeared, seating themselves in a circle on the floor of the little cabin.

"McCall, peering over the edge of the loft, looked and listened in amazement. He tried his best to keep Johnny still, yet nothing would do but that Johnny wiggle into a position so that he might watch. As he moved closer to the edge, the board on which he was lying suddenly began to tilt, and Johnny, board and all, landed right in the middle of the circle of Indians.

"The Indians were so frightened they began to run in all directions. As they were trying to push their way out of the one small door, the Indian chief hit his head against the wall and died.

"To this day the Indians have never troubled the Tallahassee people again, because this Indian was the last strong chief to keep them organized."

38. Wakulla Pocahontas

"Approximately four miles up the Wakulla River from its confluence with the St. Marks River occurred a real Pocahontas story, when a daughter of an Indian chief, Prophet Francis, by her entreaties saved a young Georgia soldier from being burned at the stake.

"It is said that the young man was stationed at a fort between the Chattahoochee and Flint rivers, just across the Georgia line. With nothing much to do, he begged his commander to allow him to go into the woods hunting. While so engaged, he was seized by some of Francis's Indians and carried to their town on the Wakulla.

"The chief said that the white man had been guilty of trespassing on his land and deserved death. The soldier was fastened to a stake, and lightwood knots piled around him. A torch was lighted, and the fire in another minute would have been consuming his body, when Malee, the Indian princess and daughter of Francis, with tears in her eyes begged for the soldier's life.

"Her piteous pleas finally affected her father.

"He said to her, 'I will let him go if he will go to St. Marks and get me two demijohns of firewater.'

"You may be sure the soldier went into St. Marks under heavy guard. When he reached the fort, the commander allowed him to have the liquor on credit. In due time it reached Prophet Francis at his town on the Wakulla.

"Many who told the story said that the young soldier later married the princess.

"I don't know, but it is said that she was awarded a pension by the government for the part she played in saving this young soldier's life."

39. Chief Tom Tiger

"My grandmother often tells stories about the Indians who visited in her home when she was a small child. Her father was a kind man and well liked by the natives of Kissimmee as well as the Indians who lived near there. When Chief Tallahassee came to town, he ate with my great-grandfather many times; and the Indian chief took this opportunity to tell many stories. Part of the following story is actual fact and the other part was supplied by Chief Tallahassee.

"There are several Indian mounds near Kissimmee which have caused some curiosity among the people. Approximately sixty years ago a group of scientists decided to open one of them. My grandmother's Uncle Ben led the expedition down the river to the mound, where they removed the body of a minor chieftain, Chief Tom Tiger. The body was taken to Washington, D.C., for study but the Indians threatened to go on the warpath unless the bones were brought back. The Indian agent had quite a time calming down the Indians, and nothing sufficed except bringing back the bones, which the scientists did.

"Chief Tom Tiger had been bitten by a rattlesnake on the leg and died. He had stepped over a log onto the coil of the snake. All Indians have something that is taken from a deer called 'mad stone,' which they claim will cure snakebite. He felt all over his body and did not have the stone. He was the only Indian ever to die from snakebite that the Indians knew about in Florida.

"When the Seminoles first came to Florida they had a big ceremonial affair and made a pact with the snakes that if the snakes would not bite the Seminoles, the Seminoles would never kill any snakes, and that bargain is still being kept today. There is big business today in capturing live snakes, but as much as the Seminoles like money none of them have been known to kill or sell a snake for a price. Some old-timers still believe the pact is in effect, as the Everglades region abounds in snakes, poisonous and nonpoisonous, and in Seminoles."

40. The Skeleton in the Tree

"Some time before the Civil War, a Frenchman lived in a little house which he had built in a tree in a field on the Thomasville Road. His companion and partner was a young man with blond hair. Occasionally he would go to St. Marks and bring back silver, jewels, and other rare items, which he got presumably from pirates whom he contacted there. He would let it be known in Tallahassee when he returned and would sell the loot to the people hereabouts.

"The young blond man fell in love with a Tallahassee girl and they planned to be married. The girl's father disapproved because of the young man's questionable companion. The Frenchman disapproved because he didn't want too much known about the details of his business. The young man disappeared from sight and no one knew what had become of him. The girl's father took her to Texas, and they never came back to Tallahassee.

"Several years later, Mr. Lester was walking over the fields at Horseshoe Plantation to see what damage, if any, had been done by a bad storm the night before. He and his Negro came upon a big tree that had been blown over by the wind. It was hollow, and inside it was a skeleton to whose head was attached long blond hair."

41. *The Runaway Slave*

Helen Atwater of Chattahoochee told me a tale about an old slave whose life was remembered in stories her brother-in-law knew, told to him by his grandfather many times when he was a little boy.

"Long, long ago in the days of slavery, Uncle Ben belonged to the Marsa of a big plantation. Now Uncle Ben had grown tired of working and he decided to stop. Knowing that the Marsa would hunt for him, he studied about it for a long time and finally made a plan.

"Uncle Ben decided to go way out in the woods to a hill where he would dig a cave and stay there. As for food, he got two little boys, his grandchildren, to bring it to him from the big house where all the darkies ate.

"So Uncle Ben arranged a signal with the two little boys. As they came up the hill to the cave, they would begin to sing in their high little voices:

You - tee - you-tee - you-tee - o.

"And deep in his cave, Uncle Ben would answer in a deep, bass voice:

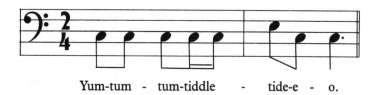

Yum-tum - tum-tiddle - tide-e - o.

"The boys would come closer and sing again: 'You-tee-you-tee-you-tee-o.' And Uncle Ben would climb up nearer the entrance of the cave, singing back to them: 'Yum-tum-tum-tiddle-tide-e-o.' This would continue till they met at the entrance, and the boys would give Uncle Ben the food they had sneaked away from the big house.

"Now, the Marsa had no idea where Uncle Ben had gone, but he hunted and hunted. There was just no sign of Uncle Ben. However, the Marsa kept thinking that Uncle Ben couldn't have gone very far, or he would have been caught and sent back.

"As the Marsa was watching the tables one day, he saw the darkies sneak some food and slip away. He tried to follow them, but they outsmarted him.

"One day the Marsa asked the boys where they were going, but they told him they were just going swimming in the pond. The Marsa became more suspicious as days went by and every day the two boys were carrying food away.

"Finally he said to them, 'Boys, Uncle Ben has been missing, and I want him to come back. Have you boys seen anything of him? If you could find him, I have some candy I'd like to give you.' And one of the boys said, 'Nawsir, Uncle Ben sho' has been missin', ain't he? But we ain't seed 'im.'

"With that the little darkies rolled their eyes around and struck off to the woods, taking another way to carry Uncle Ben's food.

"But the little darkies kept thinking about the store-bought candy that Marsa had at the big house. Little Negro boys didn't get candy except at Christmas, and Christmas was always so far away.

"When they could stand it no longer, they weakened and told the Marsa that they knew where Uncle Ben was. He gave them the candy and followed them off through the woods.

"As they came near the cave, the boys began to sing: 'You-tee-you-tee-you-tee-o.' And Uncle Ben, thinking everything was all right, answered: 'Yum-tum-tum-tiddle-tide-e-o.'

"The boys and Marsa reached the cave. Uncle Ben's head popped up—saw the Marsa—and went down again—but it was too late!

"But the strange thing was that the Marsa didn't want Uncle Ben to go back plowing. He put Uncle Ben to helping 'round the stable, and Uncle Ben didn't have to work hard no more because he had worked so hard for many years."

42. Blood on the Floor

"During the days of the Civil War many of the men were fighting around Winter Haven. Often these men would slip home for a good meal and to spend the night with their wives. One afternoon while the war was being hard fought, a Yankee slipped into the house of one of the southerners and said he would kill both the wife and the small child if the woman of the house wouldn't cook him a good meal and allow him to spend the night with her. Being a good southerner, she felt this might be her chance to do her share in helping fight for the South. She didn't know exactly how she was going to kill this intruder, since he had demanded that she give him the gun she had in the house for her protection, but she knew that if she was going to do her part she would have to find some way to kill him.

"She acted very pleasant toward him. After she had pushed her fear and hate far down inside of her, she seated this man in front of the fire to warm himself; it was cold outside and she knew that this man would want the warmth of the fire. As she began stirring around in the kitchen the man's eyes were always on her. She thought about running out to the neighbors, but had to dismiss this idea from her mind. She knew that the man wouldn't let her out of the house, and, too, the neighbors' house was too far away for her to make it with the baby.

"After a short time the man saw that the woman wasn't going to try to get away and, because she had been so nice to him, he trusted her fully. He then allowed himself to go slowly to sleep in the chair by the fire. Only a short time later the woman slipped to the side of the fire, picked up the axe used for cutting firewood, and with one quick hard blow sunk the axe deep into the man's head. The blood from the head fell on the floor by the fireside, and the house stands today, with the Yankee blood still on the floor."

43. Capture by the "Enemy"

"The sun was over his left shoulder as he and his mare, Jamie, awaited the order that was sure to come, for the men in the gray uniforms of the Confederate cavalry hardly knew but one command.

"He nervously put his bugle to his lips, since all depended on his call up and down the ranks. He had made many replies to the command, but always his throat and lips were dry until his first note echoed across the hills of Virginia.

"This boy was small and not but fifteen years of age, yet to his general his face had the expression of any of his men who had fought and killed on 'even odds' when there were seven Yankees to three Rebels.

"Then, as the sun seemed to shine its highest over the cornfield, came the even and deliberate words of the general: 'Sound the charge.'

"In an instant the sound of death roared in his ears! Jamie reared up and was the first to charge, with flaming nostrils seeking the smell of power and blood.

"Over and over the call came from his bugle, and over and over came the pounding hoofs and the terrifying Rebel yells.

"Then it happened—as it always does—the sound of death clawing, as sabers clashed and pistol volleys fired.

"Just as suddenly, all seemed to be quiet, quiet as it may seem in heaven. On his shoulder he felt a hand, strange yet familiar. It could not be one of his own command, for this grip was not urgent and frantic but one that said, 'All is over now, my son.'

"Could it be death? Was that why it seemed familiar, yet strange? Then it came again in a voice that he knew, although four years had passed.

"As his senses came back, he found himself in a Union Army hospital, looking up at a major's uniform. Recognizing his uncle, he grew ashamed and felt deeply hurt. Yes, he loved his uncle, and he didn't fear capture; but to be *his* captive deeply humiliated him!

"Next Sunday being visitors' day, when women and children came with flowers and food for their husbands, fathers, and sons, he got up and dressed on the beautiful Sunday morning and mingled with the visitors. When visiting time was over, as they passed out the gate, with them went a young fifteen-year-old kid."

44. The Headless Horseman

"About eighteen miles south of Kissimmee and about two miles north of Canoe Creek stands a huge oak tree, known to the natives as 'Deadman's Oak.' My father and grandmother tell the legend of Deadman's Oak as though it happened during their recollection, but the story mentions the enemy as Spaniards; so the date of the episode should be judged accordingly.

"A pioneer was coming up the trail between Lake Kissimmee and Lake Gentry and reached the bridge that crossed Canoe Creek a little to the south of the present Canoe Creek bridge. The pioneer was riding a white horse (the story does not explain why a pioneer would be riding a *white* horse through enemy territory at night), and he was taken by the Spaniards by surprise at the opposite end of the bridge. They took him to the huge oak by the side of the trail and cut off his head. Every night since that time at midnight, he comes back riding his white horse, looking for his head."

45. *The Haunted Kissimmee River*

"When my grandmother's Uncle Ben, who piloted a steamship up and down the chain of lakes between Kissimmee and Lake Okeechobee in the old days, made his trips, he often heard strange and unusual stories. On one of these trips he heard about the Ghost of the Kissimmee River. Someone reported hearing terrible, unnatural groans or ghost sounds when passing a certain spot in the river, familiar to all who navigated this section of Florida. The next time Uncle Ben passed that spot in the river, he could see or hear nothing unusual. The channel was quite near the center of the river; but off to one side, there was a little cove, where the water lay in a little 'dead end.' It was plain to be seen that it was just a little round place where water lay quietly, not disturbed by the current of the river. Trees and dense forests grew up to the water's edge, forming a cypress swamp.

"But it happened that the next time he passed the spot in the river, he saw a form and heard the ghost sounds. Terrible noises and sounds, which could only be described as 'out of this world,' issued from that little spot, at times seeming to come from the mass of trees, other times from the quiet spot of water. Then suddenly that little cove churned and made such an upheaval of water, as if a great monster in the water was in great pain and thrusting about. Yet the rest of the river was calm and quiet; there were no currents or whirlpools to cause the upheaval, and no river or inlet or swamp water to cause any sudden rushing of water into the cove.

"Time after time, as Uncle Ben plied these waters, he would

witness the upheaval, and hear the sounds, but could never identify them, or explain the churning by practical means. Other times, he would pass that spot on his steamer and find all quiet. Other people who traveled the river would speak of the same thing, but no one could ever explain it. And that is the story of the Ghost of the Kissimmee River.

"Another version of this story was given to me by an old-time resident of St. Cloud. She said that the men traveling on the Kissimmee River used to shoot off their guns at a certain point on the river and that the noises would start up when the shooting did. Their explanation of this unusual disturbance was that a sea cow had come up the chain of lakes and canals and was trapped up there by low water and could not find its way back to the salt water. They believe the animal died or returned to the sea during high water because the noise ceased and never returned again.

"My father has often told the following story as a true incident and one which happened to him, although I am inclined to believe that this story was passed down from his grandfather and father to him. Camping trips have always been popular and essential to natives of central Florida, and there was one partic-ular place on the Kissimmee River which was ideal for camping, fishing, and hunting. A group of men had gone down there for the weekend, made camp, and gone off fishing. Upon returning to their camp, they found huge tracks all around, tracks no one could identify. They lost no time in getting packed up and started back to town. Some people say the prints were made by a man who lived down there by himself in the northern Ever-glades region. It had been rumored that such a man existed who had had his two legs cut off and wore leather pads on the stumps of his legs at the knees, and it was the pads which made the tracks. Others still believe that the tracks were made by some huge animal living in the Everglades."

46. Uncle Ben Yates

"Years ago Orange County was one of the counties cut out from Mosquito County, and extended all the way to Lake Okeecho-bee. The courthouse was a little log house in the middle of what is now the city of Orlando. Old Uncle Ben Yates, required to pay taxes on his cattle, swore he'd burn down the courthouse.

Children still listen while the grownups talk about it, seemingly oblivious to the children's rapt attention:

"Old Uncle Ben appeared just at sundown, riding a little pied cowpony, down the sandy road. Quietly but with obvious purpose he jogged down the road. Reaching the hitching rail in front of the courthouse, he got down, tied his horse, took some light'd (lightwood) splinters out of his saddlebag and walked straight to the little building. Taking flint and steel, and his fat splinters, he built a fire under the steps, fanned it a bit with his big hat, stepped back and watched her burn. When the burning was complete, he remounted and turned his horse back toward his end of the county. All that time the sheriff had been discreet enough not to be in evidence. Men kept their word in those days."

47. Arcadia Heroes

a. Acrefoot Johnson

"His real name was Moze Johnson, but he received the name of Acrefoot because he wore a number 17 shoe. He was an enormous man, six feet five inches tall, and walked with a long stride. He is remembered for his job of carrying the mail from Fort Ogden to Fort Meade daily and figures in many stories known to the old-timers of Arcadia.

"One time Mr. Ziba King was returning from a trip and spied Acrefoot striding along the road. Thinking that Acrefoot must be exhausted, he asked him if he wanted a ride. To Ziba's surprise, Acrefoot replied, 'No thanks, I'm in a hurry today!' and kept on going. This made Ziba mad; so he whipped up his beautiful blooded horse, thinking he would beat Acrefoot into town. But even though he almost killed his horse running him so hard, when he got into town there sat Acrefoot in front of the general store calmly smoking his old corncob pipe.

"Another time, when Acrefoot's wife wanted him to go with her to church, he told her he didn't have any shoes. His wife said she didn't have any coffee anyway, so for Acrefoot to go to Ft. Myers to get some and while he was there he could get his shoes. Acrefoot started at sunup next morning and got back at sundown the same day."

b. Ziba King

One of the pioneers of Fort Ogden, settled during the Civil War, was Judge Ziba King.

"He was a colorful character and known all over the state as the Cattle King of South Florida. He stood six feet six in his stocking feet, weighed two hundred twenty-five pounds, and could out-eat all competitors. Ziba didn't 'rile' easily, but once when a wild steer attacked him he swung a haymaker from the floor and it struck the six-hundred-pound animal near the heart, killing it instantly.

"Ziba was never known to be beaten at stud poker. When some cardsharps from Savannah got wind of this Florida Cattle King named King who had plenty of money and a liking for cards, they packed up and came south. Ziba's former store-keeper tells of the procession of gamblers who would inquire for Ziba. He would direct them to the ranchhouse, and after several hours they would return broke and downhearted. The storekeeper, it is said, had standing orders from Ziba to advance the gamblers enough money to get back home on. There was one time when there wasn't enough money to pay the school-teachers in the county and Ziba handed over enough gold to pay their salaries for six months. One of Ziba's sons, Bet, is a character in his own right. It is said that his teeth are filled with diamonds instead of gold."

c. Bone Mizelle

Bone Mizelle was one of Arcadia's first pioneers. He always talked with a lisp and ended each breath with a wheeze through his nostrils. He will always be remembered for his hawklike nose and protruding chin. He was a great practical joker, a great friend of the people, and an ideal character for many stories.

On one occasion "Bone had some hogs stolen from him. He went out hunting for them and found them about two or three miles from where they were stolen. Even though the brands were changed, this did not bother Bone, and he drove them home anyway. The person who had stolen the hogs claimed they were his and had Bone taken into court. When he was called upon the stand, the lawyers asked him about how long the brands had been changed. Bone lisped, 'About a mompf.' 'What's a mompf?' the lawyers asked. 'Why, a mompf is firty days,' replied Bone. 'I thought everybody knew what a mompf was.' "

Another time, "Bone got drunk and was lying in the gutter when two men came by and one asked, 'Who is that lying in the gutter?' 'Why, that's old Israel!' replied the other. Bone, who knew his scripture, woke up about this time and said, 'I ain't Israel. I ain't Abraham, Isaac, or Jacob, but I'm Saul, the son of Kish, who went out seeking his father's asses and I have found two of them!' "

Another day, "when Bone got a message that John, one of his old friends who lived at Lee Branch, was dead, he gathered up some of his funeral assistants and showed them where he wanted the body placed. Then he took them out to John's house to prepare the corpse. Later when Bone noticed that the boys were in the act of washing John's feet, he said, 'John wouldn't let you wash his feet when he was alive and I ain't gonna have you imposing on him now that he's dead. Bury him as he is.'

"In a few years a rich young Jew living in the town died. Bone interred him beside old John. In a few weeks a brother of the Jew came from the North to find where his younger brother was buried. Bone took him out to Lee Branch and pointed out to him John's grave. The brother ordered him to ship the body north. When some of the funeral helpers asked Bone why he had lied, his reply was, 'Well, fellows, John always wanted a twip on the twain so I decided to give him a twip on the twain.'

"One time when Bone was too intoxicated to walk home, he lay down on the road to sleep it off. There he was discovered by some local pranksters, who put him in the graveyard. Next morning when Bone sat up and saw all the graves around him, he exclaimed, 'Well, if it ain't Judgment Day and I'm the first one up!' "

d. W. F. Espenlaub

Mr. Espenlaub, a pioneer of Nocatee, is the subject of many snake stories. One of them relates how he and Mr. W. B. Sealey were hunting bears at Bear Ford.

"When the sun got pretty hot, Mr. Espenlaub looked around for a cooler stand. Having spotted a tall myrtle in the midst of a palmetto thicket, he worked his way through the dense undergrowth and seated himself on palmetto roots under the myrtle's protective shade. It wasn't very long before he was aroused from his reverie by a rustling noise not far off to the right. The noise grew louder and came closer—a rattlesnake. Involuntarily, Mr. E. tightened his grip on his gun, which leaned on his left shoulder, and stretched out his legs. He couldn't run. He couldn't shoot. 'That snake crawled up on my right foot and crossed over to my left. He raised his head and looked me straight in the eye. I didn't waver as I returned his gaze. Soon it occurred to me to wave my gun slowly before him. This motion disturbed him so much that, much to my relief, he lowered his head and retraced his path off my legs and back into the underbrush.' "

e. McClellan

"Once there was a man named McClellan who was so lazy that his neighbors decided to bury him alive to put him out of his misery. They put him in a wagon and started to the cemetery. On the way they stopped at Mr. Brown's house and told him what they were going to do. Mr. Brown felt sorry for McClellan and said that he would give him enough potatoes to live on. When the men told McClellan, he asked 'Are the potatoes dug?' When he was told no, he said, 'Drive on, boys, drive on!' "

48. Wacissa Folks

The Broomsage Cemetery, located far out in the country amid towering pines, holds many residents of early Wacissa. James Burt Roach Story, born at Wacissa on February 7, 1897, and all his life a miller, logger, and farmer, told of experiences with the old cemetery. One evening just after dusk, Roach Story went with his son-in-law, Willie Gray, out to the cemetery to sit and drink a little without being disturbed. Suddenly Willie heard a noise behind him and looked back. He saw a man standing there. Then the whole cemetery lit up as bright as day. Both men ran.

William Clark, driving a truck through the cemetery at dusk in 1947, was also amazed to see the whole cemetery light up. Wilton Boland told about his seeing Roach's wife dressed in a long white gown in the cemetery, although she had been dead for fifteen years. Other stories center around a pot buried near the cemetery and discovered with $36,000 in it.

In early days Wacissa had tough characters. Two of the most pugnacious were John Bryant and Jim Edwards, who thoroughly hated each other. One day they met by chance on a road and got into a fight. Although they emptied the chambers of their pistols at each other, neither was put out of action. Their bull knives came out with flashes of sharp steel. Having hacked at each other for quite a while, they both fell to the road, still fighting. When passersby found them, they were still cursing and trying to kill each other.

John Brooks was a tough hunter who pitted his strength against wild animals. When he found a panther attacking one of his dogs, he crawled under the brush treetop where the animals were fighting and killed the panther with his bare hands.

Brooks also proved his caliber when he went to John High's home to drink. After both had become fully intoxicated, High said to Brooks, "See that door? Put it on your back and leave here!"

Brooks obligingly walked over to the open wooden door, placed his back against it, grabbed it with both hands, and ripped it from its hinges. Then, walking out with the door on his back, he carried it half a mile down the road and dropped it. High never asked Brooks to repeat the performance.

On another occasion, Brooks and Boland were having a drinking party. Brooks soon put an end to the bottle of whiskey that Boland had furnished. "Brooks," Boland remarked, "you drank that whole bottle of whiskey without even saying 'dog' to me!" Graciously, Brooks grabbed the bottle and cried "dog" as he hit Boland on the side of his head.

A Wacissa saying has it that "a morning's rain is like an old maid's dance; it's soon over with." Residents like Walter Teate enjoy the humorous tale about Mr. Greer of *Greer's Almanac* fame, who was making a trip out west when he met a small boy along the road. Looking at the sky, Greer asked the boy what the weather would be like that day. The boy predicted rain.

Greer knew the answer was preposterous because the sky was clear and the sun was shining brightly. In addition, Greer had indicated no rain in his *Almanac* for this day.

He left without taking any precautions against rain. At the end of the day, when he returned miserably drenched, he saw the boy he had talked to that morning and asked him how he knew it would rain when all signs had indicated just the opposite.

The boy then explained that since *Greer's Almanac* had predicted clear, sunny weather, he knew it was sure to rain.

LEGENDS

49. Cursed Clock

"At Marianna some years ago a Negro was convicted of a crime and sentenced to be hanged. He pleaded 'not guilty' all through the trial, but he was convicted anyway and was hung from the courthouse. Just before they were going to hang him he told them that because he was innocent and they had still done this to him their clock on the courthouse would never keep good time again. And people living there say that, from that day on, the courthouse clock has indeed been spasmodic—sometimes running, sometimes not, but never correct."

50. Family Friends

"One of my favorite characters at home is a large Negress who drives her own mule and buggy, which commands the attention of the other Negroes. Lavanna identifies herself as 'dat woman what drives dat high-steppin' mule.'

"Believe it or not, but we have one Negro working for us whose name is Virgin Mary. Her parents got tired of thinking of names and resolved to open the Bible and use the first name that came to hand. Virgin Mary was the name, but she has had a hard time trying to live up to it.

"One day a Negro called Arthur told his friend why people have palsy. 'What causes shakes is when you hold something in your hand what ain't quite dead—like a bird or a rabbit. If 'n it dies in your hand, you gits the shakes.'

"After we had completed our house in the country, there was a large hole right outside the kitchen window that still needed filling. James Callaway, the Negro who had been working on this job, still had a couple of feet left when he quit for lunch. On his return, he found two frogs in the hole. Now, Callaway was a man of few words, so taking up a shovel full of dirt, he continued his work with one comment:

Ashes to ashes and dust to dust,
Here's two little froggies done hush the fuss.

"Soon after we had moved to Marianna from a large city, we had a neighbor to come for a visit at a very early hour one morning. Mr. Bun and my father were standing in the backyard talking when Mr. Bun suddenly broke off his sentence and said,

'Well, I don't reckon you city folks will stay here long—that misery's sure to get you. It gets all the city people.'

" 'Mr. Bun, what in the world are you talking about?' my father asked.

"Pointing to some lowlands not far from the house, he replied, 'Misery is in that fog rising from that there bottom. Ain't nobody lives around here but what has a touch of it, and you'll get it too. Nope, to be sure, you won't be here long.'

"What he was referring to was malaria, but we're still there and the misery in the mist hasn't got us yet.

"One of the very old men from a good white family at home in Marianna says, when people tell him that he is buying too much land, 'I don't want to own all the land in the world—just all that joins mine.'

"This has become the standard retort from land buyers around home now.

"One of the most interesting Negroes around Marianna is one nicknamed Mooga. As her name implies, she casts spells, does black magic, and will put conjies on people. A conjie is a spell that brings about the death of a person. Mooga conjied Old Blind Joe several years ago, and within the month he was dead. Maybe there isn't anything to her, but the Negroes believe it.

"My father and a family friend, Leland Thomas, have amused me from my earliest childhood with their favorite stories. They swear them to be true, but, since both of them are sought after as tellers of tall tales, I have my doubts as to the length of the truth in a few of them.

"Edgar Bell's father had a mule that was the gentlest mule I ever saw. That mule would do anything—just anything—as long as nothing rattled in that wagon. But one day a Negro had some trouble with the mule running away, and when he returned they were both in a sweat.

" 'Mr. Bell,' that black boy said, 'if 'n that mule start to run, hit ain't no use trying to hold him. You just as well reach on back there and get that bucket.' That's a favorite tale of my father.

"Mr. Thomas told this story about Waymond's little girl. Waymond had lived on the Thomas plantation since he was a little boy and reared his family there.

"Waymond had a baby girl who was just beginning to sit up well—that was the fattest, shiniest little old nigger gal I ever saw. She was Waymond's pride and joy, and he called her Suzie Gal.

"Her mommy tied a cup to one end of a string and a spoon to the other and put it around Suzie Gal's neck. I don't reckon it ever got washed. But she ate from it four or five times a day, and what she spilled stayed on Suzie Gal.

"One day my nephew was very sick, and we called the doctor for him. Waymond loved Frank just like he did one of his own children, and when I drove up in front of his house he beat it to the gate to see how Mr. Frank was.

" 'Mr. Leland, what cause Mr. Frank to be sick?'

" 'Well, Waymond, the doctor said a fly caused it.'

"I noticed Waymond eyeing Suzie Gal on the front porch, and I knew what he was thinking.

" 'Law, Mr. Leland! Lookie there at Suzie Gal. I bet she done ate a million of them!'

"Mr. Thomas also told me this story. When Frank, my brother [another Frank], and I were little babies, Papa got this Negro boy to come and live at the house, just to tag around after us and keep us out of trouble.

"This little boy was Waymond. Why, even after we were grown men, we still did pretty much what Waymond said because he stayed with us all the time until we married and left home.

"Many was the time he took the blame for us when we made a bad mistake. One time I remember better than all the rest. We were supposed to ride several miles to the back pasture and check on Papa's favorite bull. That bull's name was George, and Papa had had him for years.

"Well, anyway, we got busy playing and forgot the errand until the next morning. And when we found George he was hung up in some barb wire dead! We knew if we'd done what Papa told us we'd have probably found Old George in time, and, boy, were we scared.

"We went in search of Waymond to ask him what in the world we could do.

"When we found him, he said, 'I just tell you boys I sure don't want to tell Mr. Thomas but I guess I will.'

"Well, Waymond waited around Papa's store until after dark. Papa had already closed up and had sat down to work on his books when Mama called him from the house. Waymond was scared to death to tell Papa anyway, so he took that time to break the news.

"He tiptoed into the store, tore off a piece of brown wrapping paper, and wrote four words, put it on Papa's desk and got out of there.

"It wasn't long before Papa got back, and you could hear him calling for miles, 'Waymond! Waymond!'

"Waymond's four words had told the tale: 'Old George is Dead.'

"After Waymond's wife died, he got to be quite a Beau Brummel over to the country churches. All the good sisters' hearts thrilled to the sight of Brother W. G. coming their way in his shiny black and red buggy—and a buggy was something not many Negroes around here had.

"But there was one thing I always wondered about. That was whether Waymond's charm lay within him or within that barrel of lemonade he kept on the back of that buggy for all the good sisters. At any rate, I know that none of his brothers were good enough brothers to get a drop of it.

"We all loved Waymond. He was one of the few good Southern Negroes left. But the time came when the Lord called him, and his funeral must have been as big a spectacle as Waymond could possibly have asked for.

"There were seats reserved for the white people; so we went in and took our places in the big Baptist Church. There were several preachers seated on the rostrum, dressed in their Sunday best.

"After a while one of them got up and said, 'I ain't going to try to preach Brother Waymond Godwin's funeral. He preached it himself while he was living.'

"And then he really got wound up and started preaching. Every few words he'd say, one of the congregation would approve by saying his 'Amen' or 'That's right, tell them about it.'

"It looked like that preacher never would quit. But eventually another man stepped up and told us, 'In a few minutes the gentlemen from the insurance company is going to pay off the beneficiaries.'

"That preacher sat down, and another stood up and started on another sermon until a gentleman gave him the sign to stop. But before he sat down he asked if anybody else had anything to say.

"It looked like nobody did; so he started to go on with the service until a big fat woman sitting in a chair out in the congregation stood up. At first he didn't see her, but someone pulled on his coattail and said, 'Sister coming.'

"She worked her way down to the rostrum, and, leaning out over the banister, told her story: 'I had a dream the other night. Dreamed I saw Brother W. G. and he wasn't sick no more. He was well and feeling fine, but it was only a dream, only a dream.'

"With this, the great big Negro woman began to sing in a voice that shook the very foundations of the church, and the congregation joined in until it made my hair stand on end to listen to that wonderful singing.

"Then the preacher introduced the undertaker, and he said, 'The two gentlemens from the insurance company can now come forward and pay off.'

"This they did with a stack of one-dollar bills. The undertaker shook his head in hearty approval, telling us, 'Insurance is a mighty fine thing. Everybody ought to have some of that good insurance.'

"And, believe me, while the preachers were finishing the services at the grave, those insurance men did a land office business in front of the church."

The great singing at Waymond's funeral reminded Barbara Hudnall of another favorite story that Mr. Thomas liked to tell:

"When we were gay young blades, we used to go to all the singings at the country churches. They lasted for hours, sometimes on into the night. And the women with young babies had a system about caring for them. They held them in their arms until they went to sleep. Then they put them on a blanket in the bottom of the wagon.

"Well, the preaching bored us anyhow, and, as we stood outside chewing the fat, an idea came to me that I thought would be great fun. We began to plan.

"It wasn't twenty minutes before we had systematically switched every one of those young ones. We didn't think the women would notice, and, sure enough, they just covered the babies up without even so much as a look at their faces. They just clucked to the mules and started for home.

"We waited. In about an hour, the woods began to rumble and folks began to holler. They were coming back for the right children, but we were hid in the thicket.

"Some of the babies got traded again that night, but it was almost noon of the next day before all of them got back to their Ma's and Pa's. Maybe some of them never did!"

Of all the Negroes at her Marianna home, Barbara loved Sol Deering the best. He had come to her family two weeks after her father had opened his business in Marianna and proved ever after to be a loyal friend. She affectionately called him "Uncle Sol." He became known as the strongest man in all Jackson County.

"If you could see him, you'd know why," Barbara said. "He is huge and well-built, although he is quite old now."

She told me a couple of anecdotes about Sol and his wife, Rosie:

"Back during the last World War, Uncle Sol's wife, Rosie, left him and went away to Tampa with all the children. Sol took his problem to my father.

" 'Law, Mr. Frank, ain't nobody home but me now. I went to the barn to do the milking this morning and when I got back to the house Rosie had done took them children and left. That boy of mine been sending her money from out his Uncle Sam pay, and she done gone with it. Right here in the middle of peanut-hoeing time. Reckon I'll be making this crop without no help. But, Mr. Frank, ain't she froze on her job?'

"When Sol found out she was not frozen to her farm work, he walked away scratching his head. Then he turned around to Dad and said, 'Mr. Frank, you sure can sleep right in the same bed with a woman for twenty years and not never know what she's thinking, sure can!' "

But there was a time when Uncle Sol loved Rosie better, and here is proof of it, as Sol told Barbara:

"We were living on the old Tanner place tending cattle for Mr. Rudolph Hinson, and me and the boys had penned the wildest bull we most ever had on that place. Mr. Rudolph came walking out with a clean white shirt on. We told him not to go in that pen where that bull was, but he went on in there anyhow.

"Have mercy, but that bull hit him and knocked him down, roll him in the dirt and tore off his shirt. We opened the gate to get him off Mr. Rudolph, and that bull run out there and start for my house, the shirt still on its horns.

"Rosie was in the yard and didn't know that bull was mad. She came shooing at him with her apron.

"I jump up on that fence and holler, 'Rosie, git back! Git back!'

"Then she see he was mad, and she reached down and gits that shirt. Law, Rosie and that bull!

"She just make it to the porch and he hooked her. But we went over there and caught that bull, and when I get his ear in my mouth I bit him up. Hooking at my wife!"

51. Hunting the Christmas Baby

Sometimes in community life a "story" is less stated than implied, yet most people live by its meaning. Such a circumstance appears in the inference that Jesus is born again each Christmas in northern Florida, where He comes to start life over once more. Like the shepherds and the Wise Men, the natives must search until they find the baby. This popular extension of the biblical narrative belongs to the shifting region between tale and drama. Bill Bunker told me about the acting out of this part of the story:

"Very old black folks say it originated in the northern part of the county, near the Georgia state line, just south of the old Columbia Hardshell Baptist Church and the Beulah Baptist Church. Most of these Madison County Negroes lived on the plantation of W. R. Wimberly, where the search would begin in the middle of December and continue until Christmas Eve.

"A group of older people would secretly hide a doll. In the evenings, community members went out to 'hunt the baby.' Suspense mounted before Christmas Eve, while everyone asked, almost as a password, 'Have you seen the baby?'

"Although clues were dropped by the hiding committee, the baby was never found until Christmas Eve. When it was found and revealed to the community, the successful finder enjoyed much prestige and distinction."

52. The Mummy Lover

The Marine Hospital at Key West was the scene of a fantastic event, according to George Key: "In this hospital, a beautiful Cuban girl, Ilena, was suffering from tuberculosis. She was tended by a German X-ray specialist, who fell in love with her but could not save her.

"After she died, he saw to it that a wooden door with a lock was put on her mausoleum. People say that he also had a telephone installed in the mausoleum so that he could talk with her spirit.

"The doctor left the hospital and lived for a time in an abandoned airplane out on the Key West beach. A couple of years later he moved into an old beach shack.

"Seven years after Ilena's death, her sister came to visit the doctor in his shack. When he left her alone for a few minutes, she wandered into a bedroom, where she saw the body of Ilena lying on the doctor's bed.

"He had removed her body from its tomb to use as an experiment. With a German serum he had made before coming to this country, he had mummified her. She was still wearing the white silk dress in which she had been buried.

"When the doctor found out her sister had discovered what he had done, he said 'If you keep this away from the family and natives of Key West, I'll give you enough money for the rest of your life.'

"But the girl told the police anyway. Since the seven-year limit for trial had passed, he could not be sentenced, but he was driven from town.

"Now in the deserted mausoleum there is nothing but an empty box. The mausoleum is closed with a concrete slab, holding a piece of the lock in it to remember. People said that the doctor would be buried there when he died. But he was not returned for burial when he died a few years later in Zephyrhills."

53. *Foreknowledge of Death*

"I worked for Miss Brown, a Red Cross field director during World War II, and she made investigations, upon requests from the Army Red Cross field directors, about the families of the boys and girls who were in the services. '

"One day a Mr. Sam Jones walked into the office and asked if he could have us investigate the death of his son, who had been stationed in the Pacific Islands. I told him that we could wire the field director of his outfit, but, as for an investigation, that would be an impossibility. Since this was a little out of my line, I referred him to Miss Brown. She told him about the same thing I had. However, she did say she would do all she possibly could to learn if the boy was dead. Mr. Jones had had no word of his son's death.

"Mr. Jones then said he thought he could probably help her. He drew from his pocket an old piece of paper, which looked as if it had been lying in the dirt for weeks, and said he had drawn a map showing where his son's body could be found. Miss Brown asked what he meant, and he said that he knew his son had been killed in this certain spot, and that the hospitals had been unable to locate the body. He even said the boy had been dead for three days.

"By this time Miss Brown was quite interested in the story and asked Mr. Jones to continue. He then showed her the map and said he had carefully drawn the location where the boy's body might be found. This rather puzzled the director, and she asked how he knew the location. He said someone had come to him in a dream two nights previously, and told him the entire story.

"Since this was such an unusual request, Miss Brown decided to follow the story as closely as possible. She sent a telegram to the field director of the base where Sam Jones, Jr., was supposedly stationed, and asked about the boy's welfare, since the parents had not heard from him.

"About two weeks later, an answer came stating that the boy had just been declared missing in action, and a wire was forthwith being sent to the parents.

"Miss Brown's answer was a revised copy of the map which Mr. Jones had presented to her. She enclosed a letter with instructions for following the map and explained where the map had originated.

"The following week a reply came via telegram: BODY OF SAM JONES LOCATED AT EXACT SPOT SO DESIGNATED ON MAP REFERRED TO US BY YOU. WIRE ANNOUNCING HIS DEATH BEING SENT TO HIS PARENTS THIS DATE. MANY THINGS STRANGE IN THIS WORLD."

T   H   R   E   E

Tall Tales and
Trickster Stories

54. *Tall Tales*

a. "It got so cold here one time that it was freezing everything. Ground was cracked open and trees were snapping like rifles. But I didn't know how cold it really was 'til I started to go to bed. Then when I started to blow out the lamp, I couldn't. Found it had froze the flame on the lamp. Had to break the fire off with my fingers and throw it out in the yard."

b. "The coldest I ever saw was one night we were out fox hunting. 'Course we had a jug of white lightning along or I guess we would of froze to death. Well, we was going along all right, following the dogs, when we ran across this fellow lying on the ground. At first we thought he was dead, 'cause he was already stiff. But then we saw his jaws working and things falling out of his mouth. So we built a fire to thaw him out, and then he started talking, only his jaws wasn't working. We saw that the things that had fallen out of his mouth were melting; so we knew that they were words that he had been trying to say before."

c. "It got so hot that it parched the peanuts in the field. Then it cooked the syrup out of the cane, and it run down the peanuts and made peanut candy."

d. "It got so hot that year it popped all the corn in the field. Then our old mule came along and saw it. Well, the son of a gun thought it was snowing and froze to death."

e. "I remember one time when it was the hottest I've ever seen it, and it hadn't rained for a month. The drought and heat killed all the crops, and, since there wasn't no work to do, we decided we might as well go fishing. Well, you won't believe it, but when we got to the river, we saw that it had dried clear up. We started to turn around and go back, but we saw something kicking up dust out in the riverbed. When we got there, we saw it was the fish; so we got sticks and clubbed us a mess of them."

f. "I was fishing one time, and the roaches eat up all my worms, when I saw a big cotton-mouth with a frog in his mouth. I figured that if I could get that frog I might catch me a trout, and I knew the roaches wouldn't bother it. So I took out the jar of moonshine I had in my jumper pocket and poured some of it down the snake's throat. He hiccoughed and lost the frog, and I got it and went fishing with it. But I hadn't fished long before I felt something bumping my leg. I looked down and darned if there wasn't that snake with another frog in his mouth."

g. "You'd be surprised at what a little Florida white lightning can do, if you never did try any of it. Why, I remember one time I was out in the boat fishing for trout, and I'd been at it all morning without doing any good. They just wasn't hitting. Well, I saw this place up on the bank, and rowed over to it and got me a bottle, and fishing was good. You see, I had the idea, thinking about what wonderful stuff it was, of pouring some of it down my minnows to keep them alive longer. And the first one I tried came back to the boat with a five-pound trout in its mouth—had caught him right by the scruff of the neck."

h. "And there I was facin' the deer when I saw a wild turkey settin' in the cypress over him. I studied a while, thinkin' which one to shoot, and I couldn't make up my mind which. But when the turkey started to fly, I raised my gun kind of auto-matic-like, and darned if the thing didn't explode on me. There was a terrible jar, and it mowed down just about everything near about, including me. And when I got up, the deer was dead, the turkey was dead, the cypress was split open—it had been a bee tree—and so much honey had run out it turned the river to metheglin [mead, a beverage made from fermented honey and water] for two miles up."

i. "I can't shoot much, but I got a brother that can. He never goes without puttin' salt on his bullets. He shoots at things so far off that he don't want them to spoil before he gets there.

"He goes up to Georgia every year and makes a lot of money shootin' the seeds out of peaches. Lines up the peaches so that he don't have to use more than three or four bullets on each tree.

"Once he got in a shootin' scrape over a girl; so he just stood there and shot the other fellow's bullets down when he shot at him. When the fellow saw he could do that, he told him to go ahead and take the girl."

j. "One March the wind was blowing so hard that it picked up everything that wasn't tied down, just about. One of our old cows opened her mouth to low, and the wind blowed her up like a balloon. When Papa saw her sailing away, he thought about her calf. He didn't want it to starve to death; so he run to the house for the rifle. Time he got to it she was floating over the pasture fence. He sighted five hundred yards upwind of her, hit her in the tail and let the wind out, so she fell back down."

k. "It ain't no believin' how it can rain 'round here sometimes. Just wait, you ain't seen no rain yet. It started rainin' one time and there was an old barrel layin' out in the yard with both ends out, and it rained so hard through the bunghole that it still busted the barrel."

l. "The finest bird dog I ever saw was one I raised and trained myself. It didn't take much training, though—that dog just naturally had sense enough to know what to do without being told. Like one day, I saw he'd pointed; so I come up to get the covey on the rise. But they didn't rise. Then I saw that that dog had one foot over a gopher hole. The whole covey was in that hole, and he let them out one at a time. I got the whole covey."

m. "The best dog I ever had was a coon dog. All I had to do was show that dog the board that I wanted to stretch a hide on, and he'd go out and catch a coon to fit it. A man came along one day and was going to give me a hundred dollars for him. But about that time my wife came out on the porch with her ironing board. Never did see that dog again."

n. "The country down around St. Pete is where the big mosquitoes grow. I was out on a camping trip down there one time with a buddy. I woke up that night and my buddy was gone, but I thought I heard him talking to somebody. I looked around and it was two mosquitoes. One of them said, 'Shall we eat him here or take him back down in the swamp?' And the other one said, 'Let's eat him here. If we take him down there, them big mosquitoes will take him away from us.' "

o. "I was riding along in the same country one day looking after some cattle. I had to get off my horse to go down in the edge of the swamp and help an old cow out of a bog. When I got back, the mosquitoes had already eat the horse and were pitching the shoes to see who would get me for dessert."

p. "The fastest runner in these parts is my Uncle Silas. He's a great deer hunter, too. Never goes out without getting his buck. But he went out one time and didn't take but one bullet with him. Well, he didn't want to break his record; so when he saw a deer he shot it, then ran and caught the deer by the horns and held him 'til the bullet got there."

q. "I seen a train run so fast until a man stucked his head out in Midway to kiss a lady and kissed a butt-head bull in Texas."

r. "I know hoop snakes'll swallow their tails and roll like a hoop. I've seen 'em do it. I saw two get mixed up one time and swallow each other's tails. They just disappeared."

s. "My old grandpaw was the stingiest man in Santa Rosa County. He wouldn't let nothing go to waste. You know what he did one time when his well went dry? He sawed that well up into postholes and sold them off at fifty cents apiece."

55. More Stretchers

a. "A man killed a mosquito so big that he fenced in ten acres of land with the bones. In the field he planted corn and raised ten barrels to the acre. He housed it all in the mosquito's skull."

b. "A man planted a watermelon vine in a swamp. It grew a melon so big that he had to make a ladder three hundred feet high to cut it from the stem. The watermelon burst, and there was so much water in it that they put up a water mill and ground three hundred bushels of corn with the juice."

c. "The mosquitoes were so bad one night that a man crawled under a hundred-gallon sugar kettle to keep them from biting him. The mosquitoes were so big and tough that they bit right through the iron kettle. The man braided their bills on the inside of the pot. He braided so many and they were so strong that they flew off with the kettle."

TALL TALES AND TRICKSTER STORIES

d. *The Big Pumpkin*

"A farmer who lived deep in a swamp planted one hundred ninety-two acres of land in pumpkins. One hundred ninety-two hills came up, but the cutworms ate down all but one hill. It grew one hundred ninety-two pumpkins, but a goat got onto the field an' stomped off all but one. This 'un grew so big that it pushed the fences down all around the field.

"This same farmer had a sow and nine pigs. One day he lost them, and he hunted and hunted. Still he couldn't find the pigs. He asked everyone, but no one had seen them.

"On the twenty-eight of March, the man heard a terrible racket in the side of his field. He went down to the field, and there was his sow and pigs rollin' out pumpkin seeds. He saw his pumpkin had a big hole in it; so he stuck his head inside. And, gentlemen! Know what he saw? There on one side of the pumpkin was ten cows and ten calves, and they had all gnawed a stall out of the pumpkin meat. The pigs and sow had been staying in the pumpkin too.

"The farmer sold his sow and pigs for a hundred and ninety-two dollars and gave all his neighbors seed to plant so that they could raise a pumpkin as big as his."

e. *The Peachy Deer*

"One day a man decided to go hunting, but he didn't have any ammunition. He wanted to go huntin' real bad; so he decided to use peach seeds for bullets. Pretty soon he saw a big buck. He shot the deer with the peach seed and hit him in the side, but didn't kill him. The hunter had to go home without any game. The peach seed, when it went in the deer's side, started sprouting. The sprouts forked; one branch came out each of the deer's antlers.

"The ole man got crippled and had to stay in bed for four years. As soon as he got up, he got bullets for his rifle and went back to the woods where he had shot the deer.

"When he entered the woods, he saw a peach on the ground; so he picked it up and ate it. Pretty soon he saw another; he picked it up and put it in his pocket. He kept findin' them and his pockets got full. He heard a sound and looked up. There before him was the biggest buck he had ever seen, with two full-grown peach trees, full of peaches, growing out of his ears."

f. *The Three Sons*

"An ole man had three boys. He was a poor ole man, who had no money and just a small place. One day he said to the boys, 'Boys, I ain't got nuthin' but this place. I want each of you to get me sompun' good to eat. The one who brings the best thing to eat will get the place.' The only things the ole man had to give the boys to help them was fish hooks, a gun, a knife, three shells, and one ole dog.

"The baby boy took the fish hooks, and he soon brought in a big red-breast perch. The ole man was mighty pleased, 'cause he liked perch. Looked like the baby boy was going to get the place; but the middle-sized boy came in with a big shoat. He had taken the knife and dressed the shoat, and it looked like fine pork. If there was anything the ole man liked better than perch, it was good pork.

"The ole man said to the oldest boy, 'Son, little boy brought in perch, and the middle boy brought pork. Don't reckon you can beat them. Guess one of them gets the place.' But the oldest boy took the gun, the three shells, and Ole Ring, the dog, and went hunting. First he found a squirrel. He shot it, but it wasn't fine enough to take his pa. Next he saw a turkey gobbler, and he shot it too. This left him with only one shell.

"He went on a little piece further, and Ring started pointing at a cat-faced stump. The boy saw a doe lying on one side of the stump and a buck on the other. He started to raise his rifle to shoot them when he remembered he had only one shell. So he got his knife out and sez, 'Catch 'em, Ring!' The dog jumped and hit the stump head on. The dog split himself into two pieces; one piece hit the buck and the other hit the doe. While they were stunned, the boy jumped on them and cut their throats. Then he put the two halves of the dog together and rubbed his hands over them. Ole Ring run 'round good as new.

"When the oldes' boy took the squirrel, the turkey, and two deer home, his paw gave him the place, for as his pa sez, 'If there's anything I like better 'un fish er pork, it's good ole venzun.' "

56. *The Connoisseur's Sensitive Taste*

"A friend of mine was quite boastful. Being a connoisseur of fine wines, he boasted of being able to name the ingredients of any mixed drink and often made bets. Mutual friends of mine

TALL TALES AND TRICKSTER STORIES

and him decided that he had boasted and won often enough. We bet him that he couldn't name the ingredients in a drink that had been made. He quickly accepted the bet, assuring us that he could name the ingredients. He was blindfolded and one of the fellows brought in a cup of 'creek water.' He tasted the drink, made a wry face, and with a puzzled expression admitted defeat by saying, 'I don't know what that's made of, but there's one thing I do know: there will never be any demand for it.' "

57. The Right Platform for the Republican Party

"It seems that during the election of 1896, Mr. William Jennings Bryan had occasion to speak in a small rural town somewhere in the South. Everywhere the Great Commoner had gone people had received him enthusiastically and provided him with excellent facilities from which and upon which to deliver his speech.

"The town to which Mr. Bryan now came loved him as dearly as the other towns; but there was one difficulty. Earlier that month the courthouse had burned down and there was not another suitable locale in the town for him to speak from.

"The crowd had assembled on the grounds of the burned-down courthouse, hoping that Bryan would still be able to deliver a good speech in spite of the circumstances. While Bryan was being introduced he spotted an old manure spreader a little distance from where he stood, and suddenly an inspiration hit him. After the introductions were over, he walked determinedly to the old manure spreader, leaped upon it, and began his speech thus: 'My speech for today deals with the evils of the Republican Party, and I cannot think of a better spot to speak from than their own platform.' "

58. Putting His Foot in His Mouth

"There were three tramps who smelled bacon and eggs frying as they were walking by the rectory of the Catholic church. They planned that they would go up one by one for some food so that they wouldn't arouse suspicion.

"When the first tramp went to the door, a sister opened it,

and he gave her a long line about being such a good Catholic and being so hungry until he was nearly starved.

"The sister invited him in. Pretty soon he came out full of a good meal, patting his stomach.

"The next one followed a little while later and had the same happy result with another sister; he gave a similar line.

"Now the last tramp knew he had better make an extra good impression, since two of the sisters had already been bothered with beggars.

"When he went up to the door, one of the fathers came this time. Not wanting to miss his chance for a meal, the tramp said, 'Father, I'm starved. I'm just as hungry as can be.'

"But the father hesitated to let him in.

"The tramp, thinking he'd better fix it so he'd be sure to get some food, said, 'Father, I sure am hungry, and you know I'm a good Catholic because the fact is that my mother was a nun and my father was a priest!'

"That tramp left without his lunch."

59. Courting Problems

"So dese fellas dey 'ranged it wid de gals how dey could sneak in. Dat night one fella he came crawlin' in through de kitchen to de gal's room, but he run into a chair.

"De ol' father heard 'im an' call out, 'What dat noise?'

"But de ol' mother she say, 'Oh, dat must been dat ol' cat.'

"Well, when the other fella heard what she say, he was sure nuff gonna look out for dat chair.

"But I'll be doggone if he didn' hit it too.

"He was so scared he call out, 'Jus' another damned cat!' "

60. Golden Wedding Anniversary

Mr. W. N. Sheats, superintendent of public instruction in Florida from 1893 to 1905, was famous for his wit and teasing, but on one occasion his wife went him one better.

To honor her parents' golden wedding anniversary, their daughter gave a dinner party at the Leon Hotel, which used to stand on Park Avenue in Tallahassee. During the party, Mr.

Sheats stood up and, glancing at his wife over his glasses, he asked, "Mamie, how many years have I been living in hell?"

Although Mamie Sheats was not a tall woman, she rose to her fullest height and answered, "Just as long, Mr. Sheats, as I've been living with the devil."

61. Stolen Camellias

Occasionally life imitates art. One of the best anecdotes I know from Tallahassee concerns Dr. Ralph Eyman, a friend of my parents, who was a much-admired dean of the School of Education at the Florida State University. Both my father and Dr. Eyman were enthusiastic gardeners, and when my father retired to Florida he became interested in growing as many different kinds of camellias as he could because he had not been able to enjoy them in Ohio, where he had spent most of his life. Dr. Eyman shared much of his lore about camellias, an enthusiasm of many men in the local camellia-growers club.

Dr. Eyman lived in the country club section of the city, which through the years had become one of the most beautiful garden spots in Tallahassee. One day while walking about his neighborhood he noticed a lovely camellia blossom that had fallen in the yard close to the sidewalk. Since it was a variety that Dr. Eyman did not have among the collection he had developed through years of grafting and layering, he picked up the flower because he thought its stem was long enough for him to plant.

The next day while walking along the same sidewalk, he saw more beautiful camellias abandoned on the ground. He rescued them also, taking them home to plant.

Passing by this same place again the following day, Dr. Eyman was surprised to see another kind of camellia in the same place. When he bent over to pick up the flower, he heard a child's voice cry out from the shrubbery, "So you're the one who's been stealing flowers from my cat's grave!"

62. The Stolen Bus Ticket

The Osborn sisters from Miami related the story their mother had told them about their little cousin Cecile, who was only twelve years old and slightly shy around adults. She had been into town to see a show and was getting ready to catch the bus for home when a rather large woman knocked her quite hard on the arm. The blow knocked Cecile's bus ticket from her hand, and as she bent to pick it up the woman reached for it also. Cecile said she believed the ticket was hers, but the woman took it anyway.

They boarded the bus, Cecile having to pay for another ticket. As fate would have it, they were forced to sit side by side. The woman left the bus first, but she left one of her packages on the seat.

Noticing it, Cecile picked it up and took it home with her. What was in the package?

Baloney, like the rest of it.

63. The Good Baptist

"One time there was a man who was a very strong Baptist and was what might be called a Hard Shell Baptist. He had always been one of the church's best members. Then one day he got very sick and everyone knew that he would die; so, before he was confined to his bed completely, he went and joined the Methodist Church. Of course, everyone in the community was shocked, and finally the Baptist minister decided he would go and ask him why he had done this. The minister went to see him and told him that he was very disappointed that he had left their church. The man said, 'Well, Preacher, I thought about it a long time and finally decided that I just couldn't stand to see a Baptist die.' "

64. Traditional Rivals

"Once there was a fabulous treasure sunk off the coast of the United States, but no one would attempt to retrieve it because of the number of sharks around. One man, however, finally swam out to it without a shark so much as nibbling at him. When he came ashore, everyone asked how he did it.

" 'Well,' he drawled, 'you see, it's real simple. I have tattooed across my chest "California is better than Florida," and no shark would swallow that!' "

65. *The Gluke Maker*

"During the Second World War, a very intelligent young man enlisted in the United States Navy. He was no ordinary person at all—in fact, he was a gluke maker. So the chief petty officer sent him to see the ensign. The ensign did not want to make a fool out of himself; he sent the man to the lieutenant (j.g.), who said that glukes were not in his department and that the young man must see the lieutenant.

"Now the lieutenant cursed the Navy red tape that caused the young man to be sent to him; so he sent him to the captain in charge of enlistments. The young man explained to the captain that he was a gluke maker and would need a laboratory and much equipment before he could get started on this highly secret work of making glukes.

"The captain, now, did not know what a gluke was, but, not wishing to seem ignorant when everyone else seemed very intelligent, he sent an order to Washington for the equipment and a laboratory on board a ship, for gluke making had to take place at sea.

"Shortly thereafter an admiral came from Washington to see this highly secret work get under way properly. The admiral himself was attempting to get a certain important government appointment, and, although he did not quite understand what a gluke was, he nevertheless thought it would be most embarrassing for an admiral to ask. He kept thinking it might help in winning the war. If that were true, and he had sponsored it, his future would be assured. So the admiral secured the brilliant young man a laboratory on board a ship. The young scientist made arrangements that his meals were to be left outside the laboratory door and that for no reason was he to be disturbed.

"About a year later the young man sent a message to the captain that he had completed his work. The admiral came down from Washington, and the entire crew was assembled on deck in honor of the occasion.

"The door of the laboratory opened, and out walked the young scientist with a fairly large chest. All eyes were glued upon the mysterious chest. The captain made a speech saying how proud the ship was to have been of service in this great enterprise. Then the admiral made a speech telling what an important assignment it had been and how proud the nation was of the Navy and how much more efficient it was than the Army. Then it was time for the young scientist to honor the ship by showing them the gluke before it was to be sent to the Pacific.

"The young man unlocked and opened the large chest, but all anyone could see was—another chest. When he had unlocked the second chest, there was another smaller one. He kept unlocking and taking out a smaller chest until he held one the size of a match box. He opened it with a miniature key, but no one could see what he picked up from it. As he held it high up in the air, a strong breeze, blowing over the deck, blew it out of his hand and it fell into the water . . . gluke!"

F   O   U   R

Ghost Tales and
Horror Stories

66. Self-Burial

One of Tallahassee's most grotesque legends is about the builder of the clock tower on South Macomb Street. It was built around 1910 as a part of a cottage, where its architect, Calvin C. Phillips, lived while his wife stayed in another house nearby. He had come from Pennsylvania, where he had won a prize for his design of a portable gristmill. His clock tower was modeled after thirteenth-century English towers.

Phillips's strangest structure was his own burial vault. He constructed the tomb in Oakland Cemetery, only two blocks from the governor's mansion, for the first burial there. The tomb stands twenty feet high, with a minaret on top and a marble plate with his last name on it. After making his own cherrywood coffin, he put it on a bier inside the tomb, where he was found dead a few days after it was completed. He had left the key to the crypt with a friend, with instructions to lock him in when he died.

His clock tower no longer chimes for the neighborhood, the fleurs-de-lis on the clock face no longer tell the time, the tower remains an empty shell since vandals tore it apart trying to find the fortune supposedly buried in it, while Calvin Phillips rests in mysterious grandeur, alone and neglected since 1911, only a year after he completed his tower. But his ghostly presence lingers on.

67. Buried Alive

"There was once this young girl who became very sick, and her condition became so bad that everyone thought that she was dead. This was before the time of embalming. Some ladies came and fixed the girl, put her in her casket, and then they had her funeral.

"After the funeral they took her to the cemetery to bury her. It was the custom to open the casket at the cemetery and let everyone see her once more.

"When they opened her casket they saw that she had revived sometime while she had been in there, turned herself completely over and pulled her hair so that in both hands she held big wads of her hair that she had pulled out. By this time it was too late, and she had really died sometime since they had put her in the casket."

68. The Living Corpse

"Once upon a time there was this man who had been sick for a long time and finally he became so weak that he was unconscious. Everyone thought that he was dead and the doctor had even said that he was dead.

"Now this all happened before people knew how to embalm; so when anyone died, they just bathed and dressed him and put him in a casket. They took this old man and got him all ready for his funeral.

"The time had come for his funeral, and they had taken him into the church. During the funeral he regained consciousness. Now, the casket was at the front of the church and was open; so when this man woke up he sat up and looked around.

"By the time he got out of his casket there wasn't a soul around. Everyone had all but torn the walls down getting out of the church, and it was a very long time before he could get anyone to associate with him."

69. Saved from Live Burial

"Many years ago there was a young woman who was very sick, and the doctors had come and pronounced her dead. She wasn't dead and could hear everything that the people were saying and doing in the house but just couldn't move.

"This happened before the days of embalming and some ladies had already come over and bathed and dressed her and put her on the bed.

"She knew that they were getting ready to put her in the casket and bury her; so she strained every muscle in her body and was finally able to move her little finger a wee bit. By chance one of the ladies in the house saw the movement and knew that she wasn't dead. They called the doctor back and finally revived her."

70. The Tallahassee Witch

Both tall tales and ghost tales are told to be believed. They are the sorts of yarns that Mark Twain said must always be told with a straight face. Much of their effect depends on their maintaining their sense of reality, of happening in our everyday world. Such stories often grow up in people's imaginations around mysterious or eccentric persons.

Rumors still float around Tallahassee about the odd doings of Elizabeth Budd Graham. "Bessie" was believed to be a witch. In the old City Cemetery her tombstone and her position of burial fascinate curious observers. Bessie is buried facing west, contrary to Christian custom. Is she turning her back on the day of resurrection?

Some people seem to feel that she is a good spirit, whose ghost still hovers about her grave. She belongs to the early tradition of a young, attractive witch. All the stories say she was a pretty woman who bewitched a wealthy man into marrying her. They soon had a baby, but Bessie died at twenty-three, after being married only two years. The bittersweet quality of her Cinderella story draws visitors to the cemetery from the city and the neighboring university campus. One woman, who refuses to be interviewed, comes every morning to meditate at her grave. All seem to feel sorry for her. Yet ambiguous feelings about her remain.

The epitaph on her monument has puzzled its readers since Bessie died in 1889. The reference in the first line to the golden bowl echoes the passage in Ecclesiastes 12: 6–7, where we are reminded to remember death in life. In the second line Bessie's spirit has "flown forever," but we begin to wonder while reading the next lines why her soul floats on the Stygian River. A Christian could not be cast aside for not having the required coin in her mouth to pay the ferryman Charon, although the ancient Greeks would have understood Bessie's being deserted on the shore.

The next lines, conventionally enough, ask us to read the burial rite and sing the funeral song for the queenly young woman. But the last two lines tease our imaginations. Why is Bessie "doubly dead"? Is this passage simply saying that her youth as well as her life has been taken? Maybe Bessie is telling us that like all witches she needed to be killed twice before she was really dead. Witches are known to have special spirit-helpers or to possess elusive souls so that they need to be killed by being burned alive or by driving stakes, pegs, or nails into different parts of their bodies. We shudder to think how Bessie's golden bowl was broken.

Ah! Broken is the golden bowl
The spirit flown forever!

Let the bell toll! A saintly soul
Floats on the Stygian River;
Come let the burial rite be read
The funeral song be sung;
An anthem for the queenliest dead
That ever died so young.
A dirge for her the doubly dead
In that she died so young.

71. The Haunted Jail

A place of haunting associations in Tallahassee is the old Leon
County jail, closed in the early 1960s. The building remains
sound with walls nearly a foot thick, of a concrete and marble
mixture reinforced by steel rods. People jailed there for beat-
ings, sexual assaults, and other violent crimes have left their
mark on the place, and some committed suicide there. In one
story, a man's bones were found in the elevator shaft of a dumbwaiter. They were from the body of a prisoner who, after breaking out of his cell, tried to get to the upper floor by using the
dumbwaiter, which crushed him when he fell off it. Another
rumor reports that in 1966, during renovations, a wall was
knocked out to make more office space and a small compartment
was found behind the wall where the skeletons of two men had
been hidden. A widely circulated account of a séance in the jail
tells of the "hostile energy" that was felt, perhaps from previous
prisoners or from associations with the Spanish treasure once
stored there. According to this account, spirits communicated
to five people but with such malevolence that Patricia Hayes,
the Florida psychic conducting the séance, broke it off. Afterward a knife and two brown beer bottles were found where the
spirits had told them to look in a secret room behind a false
wall.

When the psychic drew a picture of the malevolent spirit
who had spoken to her, individuals formerly associated with
the jail recognized him as a cruel man in the habit of picking
up vagrants to use them as forced labor on farms or road gangs.
His cruelty finally led to his murder.

In modern times the tendency in Tallahassee has been to
shrug off these rumors or explanations. Still, when my friend
Robert Mahoney Boggs investigated the jail in the fall of 1981,
he met a worker named Richard who told him about an expe-

rience in the jail when he went there to store some materials from the state archives. As the man paused to rest on his way up from the basement, he felt a tap on his shoulder and turned— but no one was there. He fled in a fright. Tales of being pushed on the stairs or brushed by in the hallways have also circulated.

Several strange events have happened to Steve Lewis, analyst of Record Management Services for the Bureau of Archives and Record Management. A self-described skeptic before he spent some unusual nights in the building, Lewis admitted to Boggs that he couldn't explain the odd pounding, as if with a sledge-hammer, on a wall behind him one night. He thought the wall would crack, but next morning when he looked at the other side, there wasn't a mark on it.

Lewis was working late another night when he heard strange noises at about 2:30 A.M. As he turned a corner to investigate their source, he watched a cell door open, then stop, and close again. This door, Boggs observed, is made of over one hundred pounds of solid steel bars, which only gale-force winds could blow open.

Boggs says that the old building is high in the positive ions that act negatively on inhabitants so that they may suffer from depression, lethargy, and illness. Probably imaginations can go wild in an empty jail, dark and damp, where rooms can act as echo chambers, or where extreme changes in temperature within the old structures can cause strange sounds. Nevertheless, the old jail is not the best place to spend the night.

72. The Music Lover

"At a girls' school, the music students had to practice organ lessons in a nearby chapel because the school didn't have its own organ.

"One night a girl was playing the church organ, over which a mirror was hanging. When she happened to look up, she saw the reflection of an old man standing at the back of the church, watching her.

"She became frightened because the man had long flowing hair down to his shoulders, and his eyes seemed to burn holes through her.

"When she stopped playing, he came toward her with his arms outstretched as if to grab her.

"She started playing again, and the old man stopped. Afraid

of what he might do if she stopped the music, she played all night long before someone came to find her.

"By then the girl had solid white hair from fright.

"Later her rescuers found out that the old man had escaped from a prison and only music could quiet him when he was in a rage."

73. The Face on the Windowpane

"Once upon a time there was this family who had a very beautiful young daughter. There was to be a big dance one night, and she had planned for many months to go. Since the weather that day and night had been terrible, the family decided that she had better not go.

"It made the girl very mad and she ran up to her room. That night she was sitting before her mirror brushing her long hair and crying, when lightning struck and killed her.

"From that day until now, one of the windows in her bedroom has the impression of her head and hair on it. They have changed the windowpane time after time but the impression always returns, and now they have painted the impression and completed the picture."

74. Room for One More

"There was once a girl who lived in Atlanta, Georgia, and one night after she had gone to bed she saw a man's face at her window. She could see the face very clearly and could tell that he had a white beard and white hair. She went and told her parents what she had seen, but they didn't believe her and told her to go back to bed. When she went back to her bedroom, the face was still at the window, and it said, 'There's room for one more,' and then disappeared.

"The next night the same face came back to her bedroom window, and this time she made her parents come in her room, but they couldn't see anything and thought that she was just seeing things. After they left the voice said, 'There's room for one more,' and then it vanished.

"The next night the same thing happened.

"On the fourth day she left for New York, and the first night she was there the same face returned to her hotel window and said the same thing and then disappeared.

"The next day she went in this big building and was fixing to get on this crowded elevator when she saw the elevator operator, who was the same man that she had seen at her window, and he said, 'There's room for one more,' and she would not get on the elevator and went flying out of the building. When the elevator reached the sixteenth floor, the cable broke and everyone on it was killed."

75. The Fraternity Initiation

"A man on a bus seated by my friend's friend supposedly began a conversation, which soon got around to this story. He told of a fraternity initiation that took place on a December third, many years ago. The pledges were taken out to a so-called haunted house miles from anyone, tied up, and left there for an unreasonable amount of time.

"One of the boys couldn't stand it and went crazy. He broke loose and killed the other two boys still tied fast.

"Every year since that happened one of the members of that frat has gone mad on December third. The first year after, one of the frat brothers went crazy and killed his wife; the next year one of them ran over another of them; this went on and on with the consequences getting gradually worse every year. The man on the bus ends by saying that he is the only one of the original group left."

76. Effects from a Skylight

"One never knows what college life will bring about, and I know of two girls who will never forget their experiences of one evening during their Christmas holidays while they were at school.

"It just so happened that these two girls lived too far away from school to return home for the holidays, so were staying in the dormitory for that little while. It is true that there was a caretaker in the dormitory, so there was little need for concern, but you know how frightened girls can get at times.

"Well, anyway, these two girls had a third roommate who

had gone home for the holidays. These three had been almost inseparable; so when the third one left, the two decided to do nothing without each other. Yes, they were that afraid.

"One night one of the girls woke up and heard some confusion downstairs and decided to go down without waking up her roommate. She climbed out of bed, but her roommate heard her and asked her where she was going. She said for a drink of water; so her roommate went back to sleep.

"Through this large dormitory was a skylight, which shone all the way through the building. On the ground floor it caused one large circle of light, and at night this was particularly so, for the spotlight from another dormitory hit the skylight in such a way that the light was directed immediately downwards, causing this one complete ray of light. The stairs of this dormitory were made to wind around this skylight, and as one comes down the stairs, a reflection is cast on the opposite side of the stairs when an object is on them below. Quite frequently, the object is given a very distorted look in the shadow, and the spaces around the stairs cause a sound to come forth as a moan.

"When the second girl awoke several hours later, she discovered her roommate was not in the room; so she went to look for her. She went to the stairs, but saw no one. She was naturally a very easily frightened person and was quite leery of descending the full length of the stairs. When a shadow appeared on the wall opposite her, immediately followed by a moan directly beneath her on the stairs, she became so frightened that she could hardly move. She gathered all her strength and literally flew back to the room, jumped into bed and pulled the sheets over her head. Whether crying, shock, or nervous tension put her to sleep, I guess we'll never know, but she did finally calm down enough and dropped off to sleep. When she awoke several hours later, she still had the sheet over her head, but felt as if there was a terrific weight on her body, holding her chest, arms, and head down. Try as she might, she could not lift her shoulders. After much ado, she was finally able to use her hands enough to pull the sheet down.

"The next morning the caretaker found this girl still in bed, her hair was snow white, and she was babbling like an idiot. On her shoulders lay the body of her roommate. The roommate's head was clotted with blood from a knock on the head, and from all investigations that were made, she had been struck several hours previously on the first floor and she had exerted all the strength she had to get back to her roommate for help. There she fell dead.

"It was also found that someone had broken in and stolen the silver, the sound which caused the first girl to awaken. The shadow on the wall and the moan that frightened the second girl had evidently been her roommate, attempting to get back to the room.

"You, no doubt, are wondering how we know so much of the story, but this girl was treated for mental disorders after the accident and recovered enough to tell us, in her mental ramblings, of the story. No, she will never forget it, for although she still lives, she is an inmate in a sanitorium; the third roommate, who was not there, told me just the other day. She is the other one who will never forget the experiences of which she could have been a part in a college dormitory."

77. *The Cadaver Arm*

"There was a girl at some university which also had a medical school on the campus. She was known by all of the students for her practical jokes, and everyone soon became tired of them. Once a bunch of students got together and decided to end her pranks once and for all. One of them was a medical student; so they went over to the laboratory and got a human arm. They took it up to her room and tied it to her light cord late one afternoon.

"The next day they looked for her on campus to see how she took it. Since no one saw her that day or the next, they decided to go to her room.

"Finding the door locked, they became alarmed and went to the housemother. They got her to bring the passkey, and when they went inside of the room they found the girl sitting in the middle of the floor chewing on the arm. She had literally been frightened out of her mind."

78. *The Wife Who Wouldn't Wear Pants*

"In Lafayette County, Florida, where an old farmhouse used to stand, there is a pump. They say that on moonlight nights a woman can be seen pumping water and moaning.

"Some say a man chopped his wife's head off.

"The reason he did this, they say, is that she wouldn't wear pants. Every time he came home and there were guests there, she wouldn't have pants on. He got suspicious every time she didn't have pants on, and so he chopped her head off. Then he hung himself in the house, and they found the bodies the next day and buried them there. Later the house burned mysteriously.

"Now, on moonlight nights, the pump pumps water—actually pumps water. On moonlight nights it is said that the figure of the headless woman can be seen pumping water and moaning for her head."

79. White Visitor to Cemetery

"A long time ago there were two old women who lived by themselves in the country. They were very poor and worked in a factory during the day. One night a week they had to take their corn to the mill to have it ground into meal for their bread. On the road to the mill was a cemetery that they had to pass. They had always heard stories about seeing white things in a cemetery but never believed them, but every time they reached the cemetery they thought about the stories that they had heard and hurried by it.

"One night on their trip to the mill they did see something white in the cemetery, and they ran the rest of the way to the mill. They kept seeing the white thing in the cemetery every night that they had to go to the mill.

"Finally one night they got up courage enough to go in and see what it was. When they went in, just what do you guess they found??? A sheep who was eating the leaves of the rosebushes."

80. The Bewitched Cow

"Once there was an old woman who lived alone out in the country in the state of South Carolina. The people in the settlement said, 'Old Miz Catlige is a witch and she can bewitch you. Don't make her mad at you.'

"I thought the neighbors just did not like her for some trivial reason, but one day a friend of my mother told me this story:

" 'Miz Ballantyne had a good cow that give lots o' milk. Old

Lady Catlige wuz jealous 'cause she didn't have no cow. She ast Miz Ballantyne for milk all the time. Miz Ballantyne believed in folks workin' for whut they got; so Miz Ballantyne ast Miz Catlige to milk her cow for her one evenin' while she cooked supper. Miz Catlige got mad and went back to her house in a huff.

" 'The next evenin' when Miz Ballantyne milked her cow, the milk was bloody. She had to pour it all out. The next evenin' it was the same way.

" 'Ole Miz Catlige came by the house and said, "Well, how's your cow gittin' along, Miz Ballantyne?" Miz Ballantyne replied, "Just fine, Miz Catlige, just fine."

" 'The next evenin' early Miz Ballantyne cut her about a dozen big switches from some persimmon trees in her new ground. After she had milked her cow she started in to whip the milk. After she had beat it for several minutes she looked over the hill and she saw Miz Catlige just runnin' an' puffin' an' a-blowin', like she wuz all tired out; her legs were bleedin' just like she had been whipped.

" 'She yelled, "Whut in the world are you doin', Miz Ballantyne?"

" ' "Oh, jus' whippin' my milk, that's all," said Miz Ballantyne.

" 'Miz Catlige disappeared over the hill, and Miz Ballantyne's milk wuz all right from that day on. Now, you can call it whut you like, but I say that milk wuz bewitched. Miz Catlige left that part of the country!'

"That was the story as it came to me."

81. Anamoses and Truenina

"One time ole Grandma sent Ambrose out in duh yard to feed de chickens, 'cause it sho' was jes' about dat time. Ambrose didn' wanta go, but somehow his ole Grandma allas could get Ambrose to feed dose chickens fer her. Anyhow, dis time he began to talk to Anamoses and Truenina too—dose were his dogs, and he said to dem, 'Anamoses and Truenina, someday I's gwina be real good to you. You is de bestest dogs in dis here countryside. Ah knows ev'ybody is scared of you, but Ah likes you just as you is.'

"Well, jes' as soon as Ambrose said dat, he saw two ole ladies standing out by de gate motionin' to him; so he thought he'd see what dey wanted. He kinda' sontered over dere and axed if he could he'p dem, seein' dey was so ole.

"One of de ole ladies axed where de nex' town was, and Ambrose tried to show her de way, but jes' couldn' seem to make dem understand; so he said he would go wid dem most of de way and show dem. But first he had to go tell his Grandma where he gwina be.

"He went on in de house and tole his Grandma dat he was gwina be wid dese ole ladies, 'cause dey was so ole, but his Grandma was a wise ole lady too, and she tole him he better not do dat, 'cause some harm would sho' nuff come to him. Ambrose wasn't dat easy to persuade, and he said he gwine anyway, 'cause he knew dose ole ladies would never find dere way.

"After his Grandma saw dere was no persuadin' Ambrose, she tole him to fix a bowl of water and put it on de table. She said if de water turn red, she would know Ambrose was in bad trouble. When she say dat, he kinda got a little scared, but he had promised de ole ladies, and he was a boy of his word; so he said he gwine anyhow. He decided den and dere to take Anamoses and Truenina though, jes' in case his Grandma was right.

"When he tole dose ole ladies he gwine take dose dogs, dey seemed so scared he say he would keep dem locked up at home. Dey seemed to like dat idea, and Ambrose went back to tell his Grandma dat if de water in de bowl turned red, to let Anamoses and Truenina out, and dey would come runnin' to him. She say she would, and Ambrose lef' wid de two ole ladies.

"Well, dey hadn' been gone too long, when de two ole ladies began to look even older dan dey had befo', and Ambrose began to get even mo' scared, 'cause he feared his Grandma was right. After a little while longer, dese two ole ladies jerked off dere coats, and all of a sudden dey were two wolves. Well, Ambrose took off from dere jes' as fast as his two little ole fat legs could carry him. He finally came to a tree jes' ahead of one of de wolves, and he clumb dat tree so fast it make you' head swim. No sooner had he got up dat tree when de tails of dose wolves became saws and dey started sawing at de bottom of dat tree. Ambrose thanked his Lo'd it was a big tree, and he kep' hopin' Anamoses and Truenina would come in a great big hurry. He kep' lookin' down de road, but no Anamoses and Truenina did he see.

"Finally, he got so disprit', he began to sing,

A-ana - mo-ses,　True-ni-na,　too,　Break de lock,

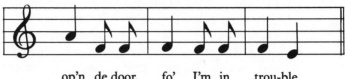

op'n de door,　fo' I'm in　trou-ble.

"Well, he still didn' see dose dogs comin', and he kep' wishin' his ole Grandma would see de water in de bowl turnin' red and let dose dogs loose. Meanwhile, dose wolves were gettin' further and further in de tree wid dose tails; so he kep' on singin', 'Anamoses, Truenina, too, break de lock, op'n de door, fo' I'm in trouble.'

"Well den, jes' as dose two wolves had jes' about gotten through dat tree, Ambrose took anoder look down de road and he thought he saw some dust a-flyin' real fast; so he knew ole Anamoses and Truenina were a-comin'. Sho' 'nuff, jes' as dose wolves were about to do dere last sawin', Ambrose called out to Anamoses and Truenina. Well, dose two dogs jes' tear dose ole wolves limb from limb. Ambrose went home and tole his ole Grandma right den and dere dat as long as he libbed, he would do jes' as she say—and he been doin' jes' dat, too. Wouldn't you?"

82. *Respect for Ghosts*

"Dey wuz a woman dat wan' scared o' no ghoses. She'd go t' any cemetery.

"Fella didn' b'lieve she wan' scared o' no ghoses, an' he tol' her nex' time she go t' de cemet'ry, stick a fork in de grave an' he 'ud know she'd been dere.

"Ol' woman stick a fork in de grave, an' she stuck it through her apron an' she keeled ovah an' died right dere.

"Dey wuz a man an' his wife trav'lin' 'long durin' slavery time drivin' a mule an' wagon. It begin t' git dark, an' dey stops at a ol' house where dey ain' nobody livin'.

"De gentleman, he tell his wife, 'Now you stay here an' I'll go out an' git some wood fo' da fire.'

"De wife, she went upstairs an' dere wuz a table wid' a Bible on it, an' she read de ol' Bible.

"She heard somebody comin' up de stairs, but she didn' pay no 'tention 'cause she thought it wuz her husband. Dis somebody wuz a ghos', do', an' de wife wasn' scared of 'im an' so he spoke t' de wife an' say, 'Come go wif me.'

"De wife folla'd de ghos' downstairs an' down under de sill o' de house. De ghos' striked a match an' he say, 'Dig right here.'

"Dey got all de bones up an' burried dem in de cemet'ry an' dey wuz a treasure dere. Dey wuz vast rich.

"Dat's why mo' peoples don' find treasures dese days. Dey 'fraid o' de ghoses an' de ghoses don' talk t' 'em. Dey runs too quick fum de ghoses. I b'lieve I'd run too, do'.

"Ol' nigga goin' t'rough de woods an' saw some skull bones, an' de bones spoke t' de ol' nigga slave.

"He go t' da' Massa an' tell 'im 'bout de skull bones dat talked. De Massa want to see de skull bones, but he say t' de fella, 'If dem skull bones don' talk I gon' kill you.'

"Dey went to da woods an' saw de skull bones, but de skull bones won' talk. De Massa kill de fella an' den de skull bones say, 'Massa got me here, an' now he got you here.'

"I built a house fo' my fust wife's muthah an' de chillen. Lightnin' struck de house an' buhnt up de whole place an' my muthah-in-law all 'cept a li'l piece o' breast.

"We put dis in a box t' take t' de cemet'ry wif' a blin' mule pullin' de wagin, but ya know dat mule wouldn' go. He jes' buck an' buck 'cause he knowed dat piece o' dat woman 'uz in dat box.

"We burried dat box, but dat ol' lady was in our yard night an' day. Dey wuzn' nobody 'cept my wife 'ud stay in dat house.

"One night we hired a man t' stay dere, an' dat ol' lady met him at de gate an' tried t' run 'im.

"When my fust wife died, she say she saw dat ghos' cryin'.

"One day my daughter an' her husband come t' see me, an' dey drove de hoss right up t' de po'ch. I asked 'em why dey did dat, an' m' daughter's husband say some ol' woman try t' scare him an' he tryin' t' run over her. I tol' 'em leave dat ol' lady 'lone; dat was my muthah-in-law. I tell ya', dem ghoses won' leave ya 'lone."

83. Specters, Spirits, and Souls

"Ghost" stories for some people are further evidence of Christianity; for them, spirits are immortal souls giving witness to the unity between heaven and earth. Among the black people of Leon County whom Arthur Moore told me about, Ella Powell had the keenest sense of all presences being here and now, including the heavenly spirits visiting earth. Ella was not comfortable in the twentieth century; she found automobiles, electric gadgets, and television difficult to cope with. One day when Arthur and Jim Shaw visited Ella, she said she wished they had come sooner because there were some white folks about their age who had visited her. No amount of persuasion could convince her that the people she'd seen on television had not actually been in her room.

Another woman Arthur knew was Lucille Shelly, whose closeness to the spiritual world was perhaps enhanced by a youthful experience. Lucille had been engaged to marry a young man who was killed by a freight train. Seeing how grieved she was, her minister said he had a job to do, and he would see it through. He married her in the graveyard while she held the cold dead hand of her fiancé.

A woman called Salew, over seventy and gifted with a vivid imagination, lived near Ella Powell and often stayed at her house. She loved to talk, Arthur said, but she didn't like to answer questions. He never found out any more about her.

Intelligent and very religious, John H. had been Arthur's friend for seven years, but he never mentioned his last name. In his fifties he worked for the Grant Furniture Company; earlier he had worked on the tobacco plantations of Gadsden County.

Independent and imaginative, Harietta Jefferson continued to ride city buses even when blacks were boycotting the buses in protest against sitting in the back seats. Like many other black women, she had worked as a housemaid. She lived out on the north end of Centerville Road.

Minerva McBroom, who could remember detailed stories her father had told about slavery days, was born in 1891. She had inherited her fine storytelling ability from her father.

Weda Taylor was something of a mystic in her own way and seemed to be living in the middle of a continuous struggle between the Devil and the Lord. Like the others, she had her own brand of Christianity.

Ella Powell informed Arthur about the ability of dead people to communicate with the living. In her kind of story, the word *ghost* has retained its original meaning of a spiritual being or soul.

"Wash Henry had done tole de preacher, fo' he died, thet he was gonna give lots o' money to all dese charities—de church, de old folks, and on like dat. Eva'body knowed, leastway they figgered, Henry had lots o' money. When Henry died eva'body had their own idee 'bout where he'd hid the money and dey all went lookin'. Nobody eva' found it, so Wash Henry's friend, Stokes Bennett, had to buy the wood for a casket and satin linin' and all for Henry's coffin.

"Well, 'bout a month after he died (le's see, Henry died in Junuary and it was about the middle of March)—no, it wus a month and a half I guess, Stokes Bennett come walkin' up to de preacher's house wid near twelve thousand dollars in silver and paper money. He said Henry had come to him after eva'-body had quit lookin' for his money, and tole him hit wuz in a big jar under some machinery in his back yard and sho' 'nuff it wus right there.

"They divided thet money jes' like Henry had said, paid for the casket, the charities, and Stokes Bennett still had plenty money left over 'cause he showed good faith and buried Wash Henry decent-like with satin linin' and all. Henry's soul jest couldn't rest in peace 'till he had put dat money where it ou'ta go."

Here is the good soul paying its dues. Ella had been impressed by this incident, which happened when she was a young girl living in New Orleans.

To further illustrate her belief in spirits coming back to instruct the living, Ella told a story about her boyfriend:

"Back in New Orleans when I wus young I wus engaged to a young man name of Henry Jones. Henry done gave me forty dollars 'cause I had to buy myself a trousseau. I didn't need to spend his forty dollars 'cause I had money of my own, so I kept it.

"Well, you see, I found out Henry had been takin' money from this married woman, she had been supportin' him, you know. Well, when I found this out I tole Henry I could neva' marry him 'cause we never would be happy wid me knowin' 'bout this other woman. I didn't hol' nothin' 'gainst Henry but I knowed we'd neva' be happy, you know, and he had done ordered his weddin' suit and big beaver hat and all.

"Well, when I tole this to Henry, it affected him a lot 'cause he knowed it was true and he said he wus gonna leave and go to Baton Rouge or somewhere else and start all over. So he took the train out and I didn't neva' expect to see him again.

" 'Bout three days later I got a letter from Brewer's Landin', 'bout thirty miles away, and it wus from Henry. The letter said jest like this and I won't forget it as long as I live:

Dear Ella,

I'm writin this hear letter from Brewer's Landin Jail. I ain't done nothin wrong but I think it's gonna be the wuss for me. When the train stopped here I had to get off and wait on another. Bout three hours wait. I wus standin roun side of the station house when this crazy man come up to me. Fo I knowed it he says do I see that switchman standin on the tracks. I said I seed him. He asked wouldn't I like to git some money an I says no, cause I still had forty dollars you give me back. He says he's gonna waylay him and if I'd help he'd give me half the money. I figured he wus lying and I walked on to the other side of the station house. He wasn't lying cause he run out an hit him wid this steel pipe, got his money and lit out through the woods. When de train come in, the white men on it seen me and right off said I kilt the switchman. They wanted to kill me right there but the sherrif got me and took me off to this hear jail. I don't know how long I'll stay here cause there's white men all around outside and I knows they wants to kill me. If you don't hear from me agin you'll know they got to me. I know I done wrong by you Ella but I wanted you to know thet I didn't mean you no harm.

Love Love,

Henry

"I didn't hear from Henry no more, and all the time I grieved 'cause I figgered it wus my fault thet he went away in the fust place. I grieved and grieved 'til I couldn't even sleep at night. As I was lyin' in bed one evenin' thinkin' bout Henry sumpin said 'Open yo' eyes.' I did and there wus Henry standin' over my bed. Leastways it wus Henry's spirit. He said his soul wus restless 'cause of my grievin' so much. He said thet things wus better now then they wus on earth and he didn't hold nothin' against me. He said if I'd go to his house I'd find his new beaver hat, I could wear it as long as I liked. Then Henry's spirit left for eternal rest. Sho 'nuff I found the hat and I wore it 'til Henry wus safe in the arms of the Lord."

According to Minerva McBroom, some people are endowed with special powers to see these "things." When she talked to

Arthur, she was constantly talking about "these eyes you sees heah in my head" and some other power of sight. She has been able to see these spirits since she was a young girl. Her first experience was with another girl.

"I wus ridin' this hoss home one day and seed this girl come out of the house. I says to my mother, who is dat gal? She didn't see no girl. She said it must have been Lorna, a girl that died in the house six years earlier."

Since that time she has seen several spirits, especially the one of her dead husband. Undoubtedly she loved him very much and she seemed to enjoy remembering him. This is her most vivid account of seeing her husband's spirit.

"I'd jus' come home from the hospital and wus sleeping in my bed. I'd been mighty sick and my daughter wus sleeping in the next room. I woke up all a sudden when I felt Ed's hand on mine. When I opened my eyes he wus standin' at the foot of the bed smiling down on me. We wus in the same room where he died and he had on the same striped pajamas he had on when he died.

"I hollered at Johnnie Mae [her daughter] to 'come heah and look at you daddy.' Johnnie got scared when I hollered, and Ed he jus' stooped over and shuffled on out to the kitchen.

"That's de last time I saw him 'til he come back later on one evenin'. This time he come walking up to the porch. I went to see who it was and it wus Ed, all dressed up in his black suit, white shirt, and tie that I'd put on him to be buried in. He disappeared and I jes' said to myself, 'That ain't nobody but Ed.'"

Her belief, and it seems to be the general belief of those Arthur talked to, is that a person who sees these "things" does not have anything to fear if he is a good, believing Christian. Arthur pointed out that belief in spirits among the black people of Leon County (at least all those he talked to) is generally accepted. They spoke of spirits as though they weren't unusual, and indicated no particular fear of their existence. It was a special, exclusive kind of knowledge in which they took pride.

On several occasions Arthur encountered a story about a spirit that appeared without a head. The stories were very much alike; each spirit that appeared was well dressed in a black suit and white shirt, the usual burial outfit for southern blacks. Lucille Shelly's story was typical of this kind.

"One day I wus out to da porch ironing my husband's clothes. He wus sittin' on the porch too. I looked up and saw this man a walkin' around the house. He didn't have no head at all. He had on a black suit, white shirt, and a black tie, and I could tell it wus Col. Shorty. I says to my husband, 'Do you see Col. Shorty wid no head on?' He say to me, 'What de matta' wid you, woman—seeing ghost in de daytime.' I say to him dat dat ain't no ghost. That's Col. Shorty, a living human in the flesh.

" 'Bout three weeks later Col. Shorty went to Jacksonville wid this light-colored woman and lef' his wife and two chillen. He got mixed up somehow with some no-goods and got shot dead. I guess what I seen wus a signal of his death a-comin'.

"Well, 'bout a month after he got kilt I wus goin' to church and I seed this man come to the gate. It wus Col. Shorty, 'cept dis time he had his head on. I told my husband to look but he still didn't see nothin'. Thet wus twice I seen the spirit of Col. Shorty walkin' on the earth like flesh and blood would do."

Although Minerva McBroom never saw such a spirit herself, on one occasion her brother and uncle had done so.

"We wus ridin' in this buggy one night on the way to church, me and my brother wus, you see. He say to me, 'Look at dat man a sittin' on thet green log!' I tole him I didn't see nothin'. He kept sayin' all the way to church thet he'd seen this man and he didn't have no head. When we got to the church house my uncle said thet he'd seen the same spirit sittin' on the log. What it wus, Mr. Arthur, wus a spirit what had been buried in the church cemetery 'bout three weeks before. It wus jest sittin' there a-restin' on its way back to the graveyard."

Another headless spirit story, with a slightly different twist, is Ella Powell's:

"I wus workin' for this lady as her maid for de house. De house had one room in it dat weren't never opened or disturbed. I asked the lady why and she say it's her husband's room and it ain't been changed since he died. I tole her thet it wus bad to do thet since his soul couldn't git no rest thet way.

"Well, I wus goin' to quit but the lady liked me and I stayed on, but I didn't like it at all 'cause I knew thet his spirit wus restless. I hadn't been there over two months when one day I seed dis man wid no head, all dressed, a-comin' 'round the house. I recognized it wus her husband from pitchers I'd seen an' the way she had talked 'bout him. I tole her whut I saw but she didn't believe me, so I quit an' neva' went back again."

Ella believed that the spirit was on the earth and walking around because his room had not been disturbed. In some way she had arrived at the conclusion that his soul was still connected to the earth by the room and until it was completely altered his soul would remain restless.

Another interesting belief among those Arthur talked to is

the belief in white animals representing spirits. These animals are always large and are most often seen around a graveyard. They never make any noise and are rarely seen for any long period of time. They just appear and then quickly disappear. An example of such a spirit was described by Harietta Jefferson:

"Me an' my sister wus ridin' down Centerville Road in a buggy one night and we wus passin' this hea' graveyard. As we got dere I seen dis big white dog a walkin' 'longside the hosses. I didn't think much 'bout it 'til a little while later this little white dog comes runnin' up. I says to my sister ain't we seein' lot of white dogs tonight and she say she only see dat little white dog right there. Jest as sure as there's life that big dog was a ghost goin' 'cross the road on its way someplace 'cause as I thought 'bout it dat fust dog wus bigger than de hosses."

John H. had similar visions when he was young:

"When I wus a little boy I lived with Boss Jo Davis an' I slept in his livin' room, an' he raised me. When I got tired of sleeping in dat room I'd go down to dis white folks' church an' sleep right up in the pulpit. There wus a big graveyard out back of the church. I'd look out there plenty of times and see big white rabbits jumping all around the tombstones. I knowed they wus spirits an' used to see them all the time, but I neva' got scared at all even though I wus a young boy.

"When I got older I used to ride to see the gals. Hosses can see good at night; they's got 'night eyes.' Why a lotsa times my hoss would shy and I'd look and sho 'nuff he'd done seen dem white spirits 'fore I did."

Theories about the soul were numerous and varied. Some of Arthur's friends adhered to the Christian concept taught by their preachers. Others supplemented these teachings with individual bits they had heard or thought up, as in Salew's theory:

"Eva'body has got a good spirit and an evil spirit. When you die yo' good spirit goes to God and yo' evil spirit must roam the face of the earth 'til the day of resurrection. If you hear a twig snap behind you it's 'cause one spirit says to d' other spirit, 'She belongs to me; watch her turn 'round when I snaps this here twig.' And sho 'nuff you'll turn 'round 'cause he is yo' spirit. Des here is a fack, 'cause I wus walkin' home one night and I hears whut I been talkin' 'bout and I looks 'round. I see these five people, only they wasn't people, they wus spirits. All you could see wus der black heads and shoulders. They wus arguing 'bout my own soul. I heered 'em, an' I got on outa der fast."

In Arthur's talks with Weda Taylor the main line of thought

was the soul. This is her concept of the soul, as related to the devil and God:

"All folks has de two spirits, de good and de bad. You' good spirit is de Lord workin' in you and you' bad is the devil trying to steal yo' soul from the Lord. Yes, yes, the devil is ever trying to drag you' soul down to hell and fire. But if it wasn't for de devil you couldn't appreciate de Lord and love Him. So you see, de devil is whut the Lord put in folks' mind to make 'em seek the Lord. The devil is de Lord's man alright, even so you is got to fear him and his fire an' all. It's mighty bad for you if he gets you. You got to keep on the Lord's path even though he's trying to push you off."

A most unusual concept, related to Arthur by Minerva, had to do with the souls of dogs:

"I once heard a preacher talk 'bout dogs havin' souls to save. I didn't understand this, so I asked my daddy. He said, 'Sho, look at a dog when he's sleeping. Look how he barks, twitches he legs like he's chasin sumpin. He's dreaming, dat's whut he doin'.' I've looked at lotta dogs since then an' I know my daddy wus right. Besides, look how quick dey are to learn. They dream 'bout the same thing over and over, jest chasing rabbits an' such, but I know some humans that have such fearful dreams that dey won't even tell whut de dreamed."

Perhaps this experience had some bearing on the beliefs Minerva fosters now:

"In the winter when it wus real cole we used to keep a big fire in the fireplace. Late at night when the coals wus bubbling and makin' noises, I'd wake up and see these things sittin' 'roun' the fireplace. They wus dogs and they set up real straight. Like soldiers they set there. There wus always a big dog sittin' in the middle of the bunch. If I'd move or make a noise they would jerk their heads and look at me like this. I see them night after night and I stayed so scared I'd pour water on the fire and my mother would whip the daylights out of me. If them wasn't the spirits of dogs, then whut wus they? 'Cause I seed them jes' like I see you sittin' there right now with these two eyes you see in my head."

John H. had an interesting story about the soul, with no explanation for it and no attempt to supply one:

"One time I seen this here big white chariot pulled by these big white hosses. The chariot wus full of people. It wasn't goin' nowhere, jus' roun' in a big ole circle. Eva'body in the chariot was plenty happy, although they wasn't goin' nowhere at all. Folks like me ain't supposed to figger things like dat out. I jes' seen this up in the sky and das all."

F   I   V   E

Urban Belief Tales

84. The Roasted Cat

A Tallahassee tale tells of a woman who forgot that modern appliances must be used with care.

Long accustomed to drying out her cat's hair after washing it by putting it in an oven at low heat for a few minutes, the woman put her cat in the new microwave oven that her husband had just purchased for her. It not only dried the cat's hair but roasted the cat.

85. The Concrete-filled Cadillac

A worker in a concrete factory drove home unexpectedly one morning to find a Cadillac parked outside his house. When he looked through the kitchen window, he saw his wife standing close to a strange man.

To get revenge for his wife's secret affair, he went back to the factory, loaded his concrete-mixer truck with concrete, and dumped it on the Cadillac.

Later that night, his wife explained with tears in her eyes that the man in the kitchen had been a car salesman, who had brought the Cadillac as a surprise birthday gift for him.

86. The Choking Doberman

A persistent story floating about Tampa claims that when a Tampa woman came home to find her Doberman pinscher choking, she hurried the dog to her veterinarian and left it there. When she returned home, the phone was ringing. It was her veterinarian, warning her to get out of the house and phone the police. He had discovered that the objects choking her dog were two human fingers. When the police searched her house, they found in a closet an unconscious man with two of his fingers missing.

87. The Dead Cat in the Grocery Sack

Not to be surpassed by Tampa, its twin city, St. Petersburg also has its strange tales. A story circulated during the 1970s at parties, coffee klatches, and civic club dinners about an unfortunate cat; it appeared in several spots, but its favorite seemed to be the Central Plaza parking lot. A woman ran over the cat while trying to park her car. She put the dead cat into a shopping bag and left the bag on the top of her car while she went to call the Society for Prevention of Cruelty to Animals.

Another woman came along, saw the shopping bag, and lifted it off the car top. Hurrying into Wolfie's Restaurant, she ordered a cup of coffee. Then she took a peek inside the bag to examine her loot.

Shrieking, the woman fainted at the sight of the dead cat. A waitress called an ambulance. As the woman was being carried out on a stretcher, the waitress noticed the abandoned shopping bag, ran out and placed the closed bag on top of the woman's body so that she would find it as soon as she was revived.

88. The Surprise in the Elevator

Two women who hadn't traveled very much decided to visit New York City. After registering at a hotel, they were about to enter the elevator to go to their room when they were startled to see a tall black man in the elevator with his white dog on a leash. The women timidly entered the elevator. When the man said, "Sit, Whitey!" they were so frightened that both sat down on the floor of the elevator.

Later they found out that the man was Reggie Jackson.

89. Multiple Thefts

Clever thieves abound in Tallahassee. In one story, a woman went to a beauty parlor that had valet service. While she was having her hair done, the valet, to whom she had given her keys to park her car, drove to her home and robbed her of her jewelry during the time he knew she'd be spending in the beauty parlor. Another valet simply had a copy made of a woman's house key so that he could break in when nobody was at home.

In another frequently told story, a housemaid pretends to be reliable and is eventually trusted with the house key. The maid has an accomplice who makes a copy of the key and robs the house at a time when the maid knows everyone in the family will be out of town. The maid can always say she is innocent because she really didn't steal anything herself.

Another trick of Tallahassee thieves is to call people and tell them they have just won tickets to an evening concert soon to be given in the city. The next day the tickets arrive in the mail, and the couple spend the evening at the concert, only to find when they return home that their house has been burglarized.

90. *Treacherous Snakes*

Stories often begin to circulate when people repeat events that they swear have happened to distant relatives or a friend of a friend. Two such stories popular in Miami involve poisonous snakes.

Some storytellers insist they have heard of a recently married couple who were poisoned when the snake eggs inside their new electric blanket hatched out into snakes that bit them.

Others tell of the unfortunate woman who was rushed to her doctor after she had worn her new coat, purchased at a fashionable department store. Her doctor discovered that she had been bitten by a snake someone had sewn into the lining of the coat.

NOTES

1. Clever Fisherman

Animals play an important part in all sorts of Florida stories, from the myths of origins through Indian legends, pioneer memories, ghost tales, comic anecdotes, and tall tales. The origins or at least the locales of popular stories can often be identified by the kinds of wild creatures in them. At times they even become the principal or sole actors in narratives; when they play such central roles, the stories can be called "animal tales." However, the experiences of the animal characters are very much like the human experiences; we tend to praise or blame ourselves through the exploits of these characters that frequently resemble us.

Zora Neale Hurston used to say that her people around Eatonville seldom told Brer Rabbit tales because wild rabbits were not part of their experiences, as gophers were. Her book *Mules and Men* has plenty of gophers, bears, snakes, alligators, catfish, hawks, buzzards, porpoises, mules, dogs, and butterflies—the animals of central Florida and nearby coastal regions. In folk life around the globe, animals have been seen as children in animal forms, transformed people, or even gods in masquerade. Beasts have possessed unusual healing powers that can cure many diseases. Animals serve as guardians, guides, and protectors. They have been endowed with the gift of speech, not only to talk in human languages but also to speak their own languages among themselves. A human being always has a great advantage if he can understand an animal's speech, since the animal is often wiser than he is. People even imitate animals to obtain power from them, because animals may increase fertility, improve vegetation, bring rain, and so on. From such associations, animal figures have become emblems of societies or totem representations; such practices linger in the names of athletic teams—dolphins, lions, bears, cubs, gators, and the like. Animals in stories serve as nurses or foster parents, often doing a better job than human beings would. Women and men have taken animal lovers. When a beast marriage occurs, the creature may turn out to be a prince or princess. Some of the most famous thieves in folklore are the fox, ant, swallow, raven, parrot, wolf, and cow. In short, people have always recognized that animals are their kin. Some of their tendencies to unite the animal and the human are illustrated in Florida tales.

One of the best tellers of animal tales I ever met was Uncle Mose, a black farmhand on the estate of Mrs. William Roberts about nine miles north of Tallahassee. Moses Miles was believed to be in his eighties when I met him in 1953. He could neither read or write, and he never traveled over a hundred miles from Tallahassee. His longest trip was to White Springs, Florida, where he told his tales at the annual Florida Folk Festival in May 1954. He firmly believed he had created all the animal tales he knew. He had never heard of Joel Chandler Harris.

117

Once Mose got started on a storytelling session, he wanted to continue until he finished. He told his stories in a continuous pattern, one leading into the next, until they created a small animal epic.

After visiting Mose to become acquainted with him and the members of the Roberts family, I took several friends with me as a sympathetic audience for putting Mose at ease while I recorded his stories on a tape recorder.

The general sequence of this continuous storytelling began with *The Tail-Fisher*, Type 2 (Motifs K1021 and A2216.1), followed by Motif Q597.3, *Bees sting honey-thieves*, which led into Type 175, *The Tar-Baby and the Rabbit* (Motif K741) and Type 1310A, *Briar-patch Punishment for the Rabbit* (Motif K581.2), and then immediately into a trickster tale (Type 122Z), *Other Tricks to Escape from Captor*, with Motif L330, *Easy escape of weak (small)*. An adventure occurs in the next episode, "Eyeball Candy," that somewhat resembles Motif K1025.2, *Tiger persuaded to eat own eyes*, with the entire sequence closing with Type 1561, *The Lazy Boy Eats Breakfast, Dinner, and Supper One after the Other without Working* (Motif W111.2.6). Further references will be made to these tales in the individual notes for them.

Type 2, *The Tail-Fisher*, is often told along with Type 1, *Theft of Fish*, which G. Hubert Smith published in "Three Miami Tales," reprinted from a group of stories in the *Transactions* of the Royal Irish Academy collected by John Dunne, who had obtained the tales from the Michigan-Miami chief Little Turtle (*Journal of American Folklore* 52 [1939]: 194–208; hereafter *JAF*).

Type 1, *Theft of Fish*, is part of a string of episodes published at Dublin in 1803 as "The Foxes: A Comic Fable of the Indians" (ibid., pp. 200–206). This "fable" consists mainly of development within the pattern of Motif K929.14* (*Fox tells Wolf to keep tail in water to catch fish; water freezes and men kill Wolf*), followed by Motif K312.1.1* (*Thief hides in wagon; drops articles out*); Motif K371.1 (*Trickster throws fish off the wagon*); Motif K341.2 (*Thief shams death and steals*); Motif K319* (*Thief induces dupe to attack bees; meanwhile he carries off honey*); Motif S117 (*Death by dragging behind horse*); and Motif K306 (*Thieves steal from each other*).

This tale, a part of the comic storytelling among Seminole Indians, shows the cleverness of Fox, who, playing dead, is thrown into a wagon, after he has already feasted and thrown out extra provisions; the wolf, trying to imitate the fox, is killed. The tale may have reached Florida Indians through West Indian or African storytellers, but it is also widely known among Europeans.

In this Florida Indian variant, the order of motifs builds first to the freezing of a wolf's tail in the ice, where he is caught and killed. Another wolf, induced to make a raid, is also killed; the fox conceals himself in a wagon, has a feast, and throws out the other booty, which he hides. But, when thrown again from the wagon, he plays dead, is cast into the wagon, and steals more provisions. When he escapes, the Indians think that Machi-Manitoo has played a prank on them.

In the variant that Geneviève Massignon published from Franche-Comté (*Folktales of France*, pp. 189–92), the story begins with Type

15, *The Theft of Butter by Playing Godfather*, followed by the stealing of meats from a butcher's cart, and continues with fishing through the ice (Type 2), which is concluded by the wolf diving into the water for reflected cheese (Type 34).

The Seminoles, on the other hand, conclude their tale with Motifs S117 (*Death by dragging behind horse*) and K306 (*Thieves steal from each other*).

In the variant from Sean O'Sullivan's *Folktales of Ireland* (pp. 7–8), the tale begins with Fox playing dead and being tossed into the basket carried by a donkey, from which basket Fox can throw out all the fish. Fox then steals other foods, including bread from a bag where boatmen put him when he again plays dead.

The Irish tale does not contain any competition between Fox and Wolf, but it concludes with Motifs K752 (*Capture by hiding under a screen*) and K891.5.4 (*Dupes deceived by falling over precipice*), which is an interesting local adaptation of the trickster's death to the setting on the rocky island of Inishkea off the coast of Mayo.

Significant variations occur in the text given by Keigo Seki in *Folktales of Japan*. Seki points out that, although no versions have been reported from China and few from India, numerous versions have been recorded from Japan (p. 3). In Seki's variant, Fox plays dead in front of a fisherman's sled filled with fish caught through the ice. Wanting to make a foxskin cap, the fisherman throws the fox into the sled, whereupon the fox jumps off, replacing a fish with a stone to keep the sled from seeming too light. While the fox is eating his fish, a bear sees him and is duped into keeping his tail in the ice until he tears most of it off by trying to pull it through the ice.

Type 2: The Tail-Fisher

The combination of Types 1 and 2 in the Japanese version mentioned above contradicts Kaarle Krohn's conclusion that the thief cycle, including Types 1 and 2, developed in northern Europe as noted by Stith Thompson in *The Folktale*, p. 220.

The question of the diffusion of folktales is particularly interesting also in connection with the Florida Indian version; the Florida tale combines the adventures of Fox and Wolf, as does the French version, while the Japanese tale has Fox and Bear. Krohn found that Bear is Fox's opponent in western and southern Finland, but Wolf is the opponent in northeast Finland, with connections from Germany and Russia (Thompson, p. 220).

Kurt Ranke gives a sequence of Type 1* (*The Fox Steals the Basket*) and Type 2 (*The Tail-Fisher*) in *Folktales of Germany*, pp. 3–4. The antagonists in this version are a fox and a hare. Six versions were known to Ranke, although Thompson reported no German versions of Type 1* in Aarne and Thompson's *Types of the Folktale*. The combination of Type 1 (*Theft of Fish*) and Type 2 (*The Tail-Fisher*), which Ranke calls a more natural one, appeared as early as the twelfth century in *Roman de Renard*.

In the German tale in Ranke's book, the fox learns in the opening anecdote how the hare manages to steal a basket of eggs by tricking a woman into chasing him away from the basket. She puts the basket down to catch him, but the hare hurries back, seizes the basket, and carries it off to the wood. When the fox repeats this trick, he refuses to give the hare his share, which he had promised. The hare now gets his revenge by tricking the fox into freezing his tail in the ice while trying to catch fish, so that the hare can beat the fox to death. Here the hare appears as the wittier opponent of the fox.

In the Florida version from Mose Miles, the antagonists are Rabbit and Gator, without the episode of Rabbit losing his tail in ice.

2. The Stolen Dinner

Variant A came from a black teller of tales, Samuel Sampson, who said he was eighty years old "by the almanac" in 1950 and served congregations as their preacher on a circuit of Gadsden County, Leon County, and Tallahassee. I came to know about him from Gloria Hunt, a native of West Palm Beach, where she was born on November 1, 1928; she met him while she was living in Tallahassee.

Variant B was from Mose Miles (see note 1 for "Clever Fisherman") and formed an episode in his sequence of tales.

Type 15: The Theft of Butter (Honey) by Playing Godfather

This type of tale appears in Ranke's *Folktales of Germany* (pp. 5–8) as an opening anecdote between a hen and a cock in which the hen steals butter from the cock. In the Seminole story mentioned in note 1, an episode involves the bear trying to get the fox's honey (Motif K319*).

The German tale, however, concludes with Type 210, *Cock, Hen, Duck, Pin, and Needle on a Journey*, a version I have not found in Florida, although Ranke reports that this pattern is common in eastern Germany. The appearance in Asia of Type 210 can be found in Seki's *Folktales of Japan*, Tales 5 and 6, and in Wolfram Eberhard's *Folktales of China*, Tale 63.

Type 15 occurs in O'Sullivan's *Folktales of Ireland* (Tale 1) as a trick that the fox played on the heron, his wife, who makes butter from her cow's milk.

In Richard Dorson's *Negro Tales from Pine Bluff, Arkansas, and Calvin, Michigan* the Arkansas versions include in Tale 1 an episode in which Rabbit tries to outwit Bear by stealing his butter and making it appear that Bear himself was the thief by greasing Bear's belly with butter; while in Tale 2, as an introduction to a longer tale, Rabbit steals butter from Bear (and other cotton pickers) while they are sleeping. In the Michigan variant, the storyteller uses a jumping incident in which Terrapin saves himself by persuading the bear to cross his legs as he jumps over a fire.

Variant A, from Samuel Sampson, resembles Dorson's Tale 1 by using a pattern of Motif K2150 (*Innocent made to appear guilty*), Motif K401.1 (*Dupe's food eaten and then blame fastened on him*), and K419.11* (*Blame for eating possum placed on owner whose mouth is* *covered with grease while he sleeps)*, a motif specifically related to this Florida adaptation.

Variant B from Mose Miles is followed by a contest between Fox and Rabbit that involves jumping over a fire, an episode reminiscent of the conclusion in Dorson's Tale 2. Since in many versions Motif H221, *Ordeal by fire*, follows the episode of stealing food, it may often be considered an integral element in the more fully developed tale.

In Hasan M. El-Shamy's *Folktales of Egypt* Type 15 is combined with various human and animal tricks, variants of "The Sparrow" (Tale 50, p. 293), in a tale from the hills of Dhafar in Oman. See also Tale 51, "The Biyera Well," pp. 294–95, where Type 15 plays some part in this story, which is very popular in Egypt among children but is never told by an adult to another adult (p. 294).

3. Eyeball Candy

Type 21: Eating His Own Entrails

Type 21*: The She-fox Declares She Is Eating Her Own Brains

The closest identifiable variant of this tale appears to be Motif K1025.2, *Tiger persuaded to eat own eyes*. It also echoes, in part, Type 135B*, *Fleeing Fox Loses an Eye in the Briars;* the fox returns the next day and eats it, thinking that it tastes like chicken. Cf. Type 21, *Eating His Own Entrails* (Motif K1025) and Type 21*, *The She-fox Declares She Is Eating Her Own Brains*. The fox, wanting to get his brains out, strikes his head against a tree (Motif K1025.1).

This tale, belonging to the group of animal stories from Mose Miles, appears to be at least partly his own invention. If other versions of *Eating Eyeballs for Candy* show up, perhaps a new Type Number should be assigned to it.

Type 135*: Fleeing Fox Loses an Eye in the Briars

This type appears to be another remote variation on Type 21 (Motif K1025) and Type 21* (Motif K1025.1). The episode involves harm that the trickster either inflicts on himself or suffers accidentally.

In Motif K1025.1 (in which the fox, wanting to get his brains out, strikes his head against a tree) there is an echo of an Irish tale (O'Sullivan, p. 8), where the fox saves himself by swinging down to his den on a briar at the edge of a cliff; when people partly cut the briar, it breaks and the fox falls to his death. (Cf. Motif K891.5.4, *Dupes deceived into falling over precipice*.)

4. The Foolish Diver

Variant A belongs to the repertory of Leola Conway, a black storyteller who was a thirty-eight-year-old resident of Tallahassee in 1950.

Variant B came from another black Tallahassee resident, Ben Fields, born in Gadsden County and fifty years old in 1950. Ben said he heard his tale from his father.

Type 34: The Wolf Dives into the Water for Reflected Cheese

As already noted in connection with Type 1, this episode is used in Massignon's French version as a conclusion of a structure linking Type 15 + Type 2 + Type 34.

The actors in both variants are the rabbit and the fox, but the difference in the trickster Rabbit's farewells to the outwitted Fox are worth nothing. In Variant A, Rabbit recites a couplet while in Variant B, without using the element of reflected cheese in the water, Rabbit gives Fox a bit of worldly-wise advice.

Pertinent motifs are J1791.3 (*Diving for cheese*) and K735.5 (*Dupe tricked into well: left there*).

5. Learning to Fear Men

The quoted text came from Ben Fields, but Samuel Sampson also told this tale, which he ended with the turkey gobbler saying, "Coupla de son of a bitches dere yit, coupla de son of a bitches dere yit."

Type 157: Learning to Fear Men

The amusing Florida version showing how the chickens, ducks, and turkeys learn they can escape being fed to visiting preachers by using their animal speech is somewhat echoed in the dramatic style of an Upper Brittany tale (Massignon, *France*, pp. 23–29), which uses conversations about the devil wanting to poison a young man, who is advised by one of the devil's daughters never to eat or drink anything she brings from the devil. The daughter helps the young man perform otherwise impossible deeds the devil assigns to him.

More directly related to the Florida tale is Massignon's Tale 21 using the widespread North European Type 157, fully localized to the French setting in Upper Poitou by the French grandmother who told it.

American variants can be found in Dorson's "King Beast of the Forest Meets Man," pp. 118–28.

The bear's challenge to man undergoes an interesting development in a German tale (Ranke, Tale 7, pp. 19–20), in which the fox outwits the stupid bear, who thinks that the cat with its tail in air is a hunter with his bayonet fixed, while the dog bent over must be another hunter with his arms reaching for stones to kill the bear. This tale combines Type 157 with Type 104, *The Cowardly Duelers*.

The quality of such a tale seems to derive from the Aesopic fable. A modern analogy occurs in Georgios Megas's *Folktales of Greece*, where his Tale 11, "Cat, Lion, and Man," has the cat instructing the lion about how frightful man can be, after the woodcutter traps the lion's paws in a piece of split wood (Motif K1111), which does not appear in any of Dorson's American versions.

In his *Negro Tales* Dorson gives one Arkansas version in which the rabbit is telling the bear what kind of creature a man is, after a soldier has shot the bear in the face as well as in the rear (Tale 13a). Another Arkansas tale has the bear showing a man to a panther, who is filled with splinters from wood the man throws at him (Tale 13b). Both tales also build suspense from having the innocent creatures first meet a youngster, who is called "a gonner-be," and an old man, who is a "has-been," before the dangerous man appears. Dorson's Michigan variant is a cante-fable explaining why the buzzard is bald because he has been frightened by the supposed ghost of a rabbit, causing him to fly into a tree and hit his head, tearing the skin off. This kind of origin tale is combined with Type 157 in another version found in Dorson's "King Beast of the Forest Meets Man," Text N.

Central motifs are J17 (*Animal learns through experience to fear men*), B210 (*Speaking animals*), B211.1 (*Speaking beasts—domestic*), and B857 (*Animal avenges injury*).

The Egyptian tale called "Son-of-Adam and the Lion" uses Types 157 (*Learning to Fear Men*), 121 (*Wolves Climb on Top of One Another to Tree*), and 152A* (*The Wife Scalds the Wolf*). This composite of tale types is well known in Egypt and throughout north Africa. Perhaps these episodes should more logically be combined into one type. (See Hasan El-Shamy, *Egypt*, p. 290.) Existing evidence appears to make Type 157, *Learning to Fear Men*, less a part of the literary fable tradition in India and Greece than of ancient Egyptian oral storytelling, as early as the fourteenth century B.C. (p. 291).

6. The Tarbaby

Mose Miles dramatized this tale while he told it by going through the motions of Rabbit trying to free himself from Fox's tarbaby.

Type 175: The Tarbaby and the Rabbit
(Motif K741, Captured by tarbaby)

Type 1310A: Briar-patch Punishment for Rabbit
(Motif K581.2)

Instead of the more customary introduction, with the rabbit stealing fruit from a garden, this tale has the rabbit making the spring water muddy. As usual, the capture is followed by the pseudo-punishment in the briar patch.

This tale not only has worldwide distribution but may also have either animal or human actors, as in the Chilean version of Yolando Pino-Saavedra, *Folktales of Chile*, pp. 4–5. In Chile it appears in both Spanish and Indian variants. Another trait typical of the tale seems to be its tendency to become part of a sequence or string of episodes dealing with tricks and jokes, as in Mose Miles's tales in this volume. It is often only an episode in the story of Rabbit's cleverness rather than a separate story.

Since Mose Miles insisted he made up all of his own stories, there is little point in speculating on how or where he may have heard them. This tale can be found as Tale 24 in Elsie Clews Parsons's *Folklore of the Antilles, French and English,* pt. 3, with many references, as well as in Parsons's *Folklore of the Sea Islands, South Carolina,* Tales 13, 14, and 15. Tale 13 is worth noting as an amusing variant because the figure beside the well appears to be a girl, whom Rabbit tries to kiss. When she won't turn him loose, he explains to Wolf that she loves him too much. The briar-patch conclusion is used in Tale 14 with several close variants. Other "riddles" for tricking Wolf show up in Tale 15, as when Wolf burns the house where the Rabbit family has taken refuge and Rabbit gets away by spitting tobacco in Wolf's eye.

Dorson found Type 15 (*The Theft of Butter [Honey]*) more popular than Type 175 (*The Tarbaby*) in tales from Arkansas; yet the two episodes were sometimes joined (Dorson, *Negro Tales,* p. 16). In Mose's Florida tales in this volume we can see even more clearly the elaborate tendency to keep moving without interruption from one animal tale to another.

The version from Chile shows how the tarbaby device came to be used in human as well as animal stories. The protagonist traps someone by getting him stuck fast to an object to prevent him from stealing figs. The nature of the sticky fellow is discovered when the thief tries to run away from him, while the thief's companion cries out that a goblin is trying to eat them.

Over 300 versions of the tarbaby episode are examined in Aurelio M. Espinosa's *Cuentos Populares Españoles,* 2: 163–227. A Mexican tale told in Texas is composed of several tale types and motifs in a series of tricks, usually beginning with Type 175 (*The Tarbaby and the Rabbit*), but not necessarily.

The most frequent ending, however, is Type 34, *The Wolf Dives into the Water for Reflected Cheese.*

See Américo Paredes, *Folktales of Mexico,* p. 212.

7. *Learning What Fear Is*

Barbara Hudnall told me this tale in the fall of 1949 as she had heard it from her mother, who had learned it from an elderly black in Georgia. Born in Birmingham, Alabama, in 1929, Barbara was a transplant who had adopted Marianna, Florida, as her hometown.

Type 326: The Youth Who Wanted To Learn What Fear Is

This kind of ghost story involves a great variety of motifs, since many means of creating fear are used to scare the careless or naive human being. Among them are E281, *Ghosts haunt house,* and E423.1.2, *Revenant as cat,* both of which appear in these Florida tales. The ghostly cat often puts in an appearance to educate the inexperienced youth into the terrors of an unknown world.

"Yann the Fearless," from Lower Brittany, is one among many French ghost tales from several provinces (Massignon, *France,* pp. 3–8). French immigrants have brought it into Canada, Michigan, and Missouri. The length of the tale seems to depend on the fruitfulness

of the storyteller in mustering one frightful appearance after another—
or perhaps on the credulity of the audience.

Although the nineteenth-century Grimm collection is usually given
credit for presenting the first European version of Type 326, we know
it was familiar to seventeenth-century Frenchmen (Massignon, *France,*
p. 247). The idea of a revenant is employed in both Florida and French
tales to test the protagonist's courage at the same time that the ghost
leads to the hidden or buried treasure.

The motifs of *Dismembered corpse* (E422.1.10), *Revenant as face or
head* (E422.1.11.2), *Ghost as head or hands* (E422.1.11.3), and the like
appear throughout Florida tales. They may also play a part in Type
325, *The Magician and His Pupil;* an interesting Japanese version is in
Seki, *Japan,* Tale 31. The corpse or some of its members falling into
food or cooking utensils as an episode in Type 326 can be found in the
Arkansas tale from Dorson, *Negro Tales,* pp. 76–78, as a comic incident. Adventures in a haunted house occur in the same Dorson collection (pp. 78–81). A striking version in which various parts of a man
fall from overhead, until they unite to form a giant with fourteen
heads, was told to Elsie Clews Parsons by a Portuguese black (*Folklore
from the Cape Verde Islands,* pp. 241–44).

Featured motifs in this Florida version are D342, *Transformation:
cat to person,* and E521.3, *Ghost as cat.*

8. Katie and Johnnie

This version of "Hansel and Gretel" came to me from Sidney Grovenstein, a native of West Palm Beach, Florida, where he was born in
1926; his father, W. D. Grovenstein, told it to him. I knew Sidney as
a teller of tales from 1950 to 1954.

Type 327A: Hansel and Gretel

The Florida version of this widely distributed tale has several interesting characteristics. It belongs to the typically European tale complex
in which a parent, who may be kind but poor, sends the children away.
According to Seki (*Japan,* p. 51), most Japanese tales have a wicked
stepmother as villain; yet in the version entitled "Oni and the Three
Children" (pp. 51–54) the children are abandoned by their real mother.
Although cruel stepmothers drive children from home in both European and Oriental tales, the Florida tale has the motivation of the tale
depending on the mother, who sends the brother and sister to get
switches for brooms to sweep their yard. This story is set in south
Georgia, and the large size of the backyards on Georgia farms is
mentioned, a vivid local detail. Instead of being trapped by a witch in
a gingerbread house, the Katie and Johnnie of this tale are tempted to
eat cakes hanging from a tree, from which the giant's cage falls down
upon them. They successfully escape from the cage and lock the giant
in it, an example of Motif G514.1, *Ogre trapped in box (cage).* They
then drown him in the river. The children, fearing they have gone too

far into the Georgia swamps, are afraid of being punished but are welcomed home with kisses.

In the Japanese tale, which may well belong to independently invented stories of this type, the mother feels she must take her children to the mountains because she is too poor to care for her three boys. (There is no "Gretel" here.) The ogre that the boys must face is the Japanese *oni*. Like other giants, the *oni* has a good sense of smell and sniffs the human odor of the boys in an underground storage pit, where they have been hidden by the old woman staying with the *oni*. The children escape by stealing the *oni*'s boots, which can cover over 2,000 miles in one step.

Throughout these versions the monster's appetite for eating children is constant.

In the tale known as "The Little Guava" from Tlaxcala, Mexico, the children's father abandons them in the woods because their stepmother is tired of them, but they succeed at first in finding their way home because the boy had dropped guava peelings along the way and the girl had scattered ashes she had hidden in her pocket. When the father deserts them a second time, the children have further adventures, including stealing pancakes from an old woman and being fattened for sale because they are mistaken for hogs. A lady finally rescues them by giving them animals on which to ride back home (Paredes, *Mexico*, Tale 31).

9. Outwitting the Giant

Type 328: The Boy Steals the Giant's Treasure

Cognate with many stories that tell of someone who attempts to get even for former abuses or who merely happens to come upon a giant, this Florida trickster tale belongs to the British cycle of Jack tales. Localized from family tradition in Georgia, the tale begins casually with Jack happening to meet a giant who boasts of his strength. Being small but clever, Jack puts the giant through some tests of strength just for fun; for example, the stupid ogre (Motif G501) is challenged to squeeze liquid from a rock (Motif K62). Instead of stealing treasure, Jack steals the giant's pride. This sort of tale overlaps with Type 327G, as well as part of Type 328, in which the ogre is deceived in some way.

The complexities of interrelated types become particularly apparent in the Chinese tale "The Wang-liang's Magic Cap" (Eberhard, *China*, Tale 43, pp. 95–96).

Only remotely related to the Florida tale, the Chinese story achieves its main effects from the protective devices a character may employ against the Chinese ogre Wang-liang, such as holding some sort of stick in front of himself, with one point against his breast and the other end pointed at the ogre. This position prevents the monster from moving. Various tricks of this nature are used to control the ogre.

Having rendered the ogre helpless, a young Chinaman, A San, demands the ogre's straw hat, which has the magic power to make its wearer invisible. From this point, tricksters trick tricksters, for A San begins stealing from fruit stalls while he wears his magic cap until another Wang-liang sees him and steals his cap.

The sequence continues with another man, A Lin, who, after capturing a Wang-liang, demands the skin from his face, which serves as a magic mask, making the wearer invisible. Later he takes a magic cap from another ogre. He also becomes a thief, stealing jewelry and silver until he becomes rich. He is thwarted when his wife mistakes the cap for rice straw and uses it as fuel. Turning to gambling, he finally loses his mask when his luck turns against him.

In this kind of story, the emphasis is less on stealing from a giant or monster than on the stealing that the character does afterward.

An even more complex narrative occurs in the Hungarian tale known as "The Story of the Gallant Szerus" (Linda Dégh, *Folktales of Hungary*, Tale 8, pp. 109–26). It is a mosaic of several tale types interwoven in a long *märchen*. Type 328, dealing with stealing treasure, is only one motivating episode in this conglomerate of Types 590, 400, 313, 531, and 300. A series of individual tales was perhaps combined in this way to hold the listeners' attention; the narrative came from a miner, who, walking with his fellow workers many miles each way to and from the mine, used the telling of tales to shorten the walk.

In *Folktales of Egypt*, Hasan El-Shamy records further complexities appearing in African tales, including a Bantu version from the area of the Cape of Good Hope that combines elements from Type 328 with Type 1655 ("The Profitable Exchange," p. 293).

Type 1060: Squeezing the (Supposed) Stone

In British and American stories this trick may be among the adventures of the hero Jack. Richard Dorson published a version of it from North Carolina in *Buying the Wind* (pp. 168–72).

A Greek variant is widely known in various parts of the country where modern Greeks believe in the *drakos*, a huge, strong ogre appearing in human form. The *drakos* is outwitted by "baldchin," who has scattered pieces of cheese among the stones. This Greek tale proceeds with a number of other tricks (Megas, *Greece*, Tale 57, pp. 172–76).

In the Florida tale of Jack and the giant, the squeezing of the supposed stone is followed by only one other trick to fool the giant (Type 1062).

Type 1062: Throwing the Stone (Motif K18.3, Throwing contest: bird substituted for stone)

As noted above for Type 1060, this episode closes the Florida tale of Jack and the giant. In Type 1062, the bird is substituted for the stone so that the supposed stone is thrown out of sight. In Megas, *Greece*, Type 1063B appears in the rivalry because the *drakos* fears having the ball thrown to Constantinople and Smyrna, where his sisters live (Tale 57). All such incidents of course turn up in cycles of contests won by deception.

The Florida tale was part of the set of Jack stories told me by Sidney Grovenstein of West Palm Beach, Florida. (See Tale 8.)

10. Old Tor

This tale of the fearful threat to children was told me by Marie Locklin, born in Key West, Florida, in 1936; she lived in Jay, Florida, from 1955 to 1959, when I knew her. Big Tor was known to the children in Jay.

Such a story belongs to the complex of "Bloody Bones" types of tales to scare children. Big Tor also is related to the big bad wolf of the Red Riding Hood tradition.

Type 333: The Glutton

In the Florida tale of a glutton, the threatening Big Tor tries to capture mischievous children, whom he probably will eat in true folk fashion. The story, however, is a comic ghost tale, in which the suspense is finally broken when the trembling children see the joke.

Deceptive appearances seem to play a more serious role in the French version; "Boudin-Boudine" is a variant of "Little Red Riding Hood," featuring a boy instead of a girl (Massignon, *France*, Tale 16, pp. 74–76). The wolf threatens the grandmother, but she is too sharp for him and succeeds in keeping him from entering. On the way back home, the boy meets his father searching for him, the wolf is killed, and the boy happily wears the wolf's skin. All ends well except for the wolf.

The happy ending, different from Perrault's version best known to Americans, is found in various sections of France, Italy, and Tyrol. Whether American children have been more entertained by the conclusion in *Mother Goose's Tales* of the wolf gobbling up Little Red Riding Hood remains moot. In any event, I've never heard the moral of the well-intentioned Charles Perrault story attached to versions in the United States, but children or adults might benefit from being reminded that "these smooth-tongued, smooth-pelted wolves are the most dangerous beasts of all" (*The Fairy Tales of Charles Perrault*, p. 28). See also "Le petit chaperon rouge" ("Little Red Riding Hood") and "Cendrillon, ou la petite pantoufle de verre" ("Cinderella") in Perrault's *Histoires, ou contes du temps passé, avec des moralités* (Paris: Claude Barbin, 1697).

A detail that relates the French story to the Florida one is that Perrault suggests the acting out of the threats in a marginal note of his manuscripts. In addition, Angela Carter, the translator of the Avon edition, mentions that her English grandmother always pounced with a roar at the end when the wolf gets the girl ("Introduction," p. 13).

Among Japanese tales, "The Golden Chain from Heaven" (Seki, *Japan*, Tale 21, pp. 54–57) furnishes further twists to the "Red Riding Hood" complex. Japanese tales usually have only human actors. But in this tale the Japanese ogre, Yamauba, somewhat resembles the Florida "Big Tor" because both are frightening figures who threaten children, yet Yamauba is also a stupid ogre defeated by impulsiveness. However, the trick of the villain trying to disguise its hands is preserved in both the Massignon and the Seki texts. Still, the Japanese keep a somewhat happy ending since the children are transformed into a moon and a star after the ogre's death.

Because of its structure, the Florida tale relates to Motif Z18.1 (*Formulistic conversations: What makes your ears so big? etc.*), as well as to Motif Z46.1* (*Continuous threats mount*).

11. The Witch's Curse

The violent response of a witch denied the child she wants is the focus of this tale from Barbara (Boots) Haynie, born in 1945. She was a specialist in Clearwater tales, although her residence when I knew her during 1963 was in Fort Lauderdale, Florida.

Type 410: Sleeping Beauty

The Florida tale follows only in some respects the main outline of the "Sleeping Beauty" type: the wished-for child, the gift of a child, the threat against the child, and the vain attempts to escape the curse. But, instead of a prince breaking the curse of eternal sleep or death, the girl eventually dies "from a horse's hoof," which turns out to be a hole made by a hoof, a hole that has the power of mysteriously strangling her.

Central motifs are N2.6.2 (*Daughter as wager*), G269.4 (*Curse by disappointed witch*), K940 (*Deception into killing own family or animals*), M370 (*Vain attempts to escape fulfillment of prophecy*), M412.1 (*Curse given at birth of child*), and S113 (*Murder by strangling*).

In the South American version given in Pino-Saavedra's collection of folktales from Chile, the conventional motivation of apparent death caused by pricking a finger sets the tale in motion. Expansions of the well-known Grimm or Perrault versions build this tale through episodes of frustrated cannibalism when the jealous queen tries to have the king eat his son and daughter, who are children born from the no-longer-sleeping beauty. When the queen invites the beauty to the palace to kill her, the beauty puts on her dress trimmed with little bells to prepare for death; as the king had promised her, he hears the bells and saves her.

Since so many of the violent themes typical of either Germanic or Romance variants have dropped entirely out of the Florida tale, we must wonder whether it is only a faint memory of some Spanish, Italian, or French tale. It may be a separate creation about expressing wishes and rashly making agreements with someone like the witch who demands a favor in return if she consents to use her power to grant the wish.

Fantastic elements from Arthurian romances are reflected in the French version (Massignon, *France*, Tale 37, pp. 133–35), describing the castle of the seven-headed monster defeated by King Arthur's son so that he can marry the girl, still young though over a hundred years old, who has been kept waiting by her godmother until the right man appears to resuscitate and marry her. One graphic realistic effect is included at the end of this version from Ambérac (Angoumois): the enchanted castle (which had been surrounded with trees, brambles, and thorns in Perrault's tale) still stands in a great forest, but only a part of the high ruined wall can be seen.

12. Peazy and Beanzy

During the 1950s and 1960s this tale became known to young women who were patients in the Florida State University infirmary. It was told them by an elderly black attendant, who wished to remain anonymous but claimed the story came from Louisiana, where her mother had told it to her. This version was related to me by Virginia Spencer of West Palm Beach as she remembered hearing it.

It relies on Motifs N827 (*Child as helper*) and N831 (*Girl as helper*), but especially Motif L54 (*Compassionate youngest daughter*), with its central structure depending on Motif Q2 (*Kind and unkind*).

It reflects elements of Types 431, 480, and 620.

Type 431: The House in the Wood

The Florida version from the elderly Tallahassee woman occurs in a fully southern setting. Instead of the usual three girls, two sisters act out the popular motif of the kind and the unkind. This story is not merely a retelling of the Grimms' tale. The identification of this narrative apparently depends on whether the focus is placed on the distinctive destination of the journey or on the special qualities of the people and their behavior. "The House in the Wood" describes thoughtless behavior toward such animals as a cock, a hen, and a cow. The youngest girl breaks their enchantment by feeding them, and the old man taking care of them turns out to be a prince, who of course marries the kind girl. The Florida version emphasizes the sisters' household tasks as well as their attitudes toward nature. (See Type 480.)

Type 480: The Spinning-Woman by the Spring; The Kind and the Unkind Girls

The Florida version lacks the introductory episode of the despised youngest daughter spinning by a well, into which she drops her shuttle; she must jump into the well to find it, in a mysterious lower world. This episode can constitute the sole story, as it does in the Grimms' "Frau Holle," where the plot turns on the contrasting behavior of the older daughters in the lower world. All such tales belong to the famous "Cinderella" cycle.

The special quality of the Florida tale derives from its feeling for nature, represented by the brook and the plum tree, which Peazy neglects and Beanzy nurtures.

An English tale contains similar episodes (see Katherine M. Briggs and Ruth L. Tongue, *Folktales of England*, Tale 2). This kind of tale is studied in full by Anna B. Rooth in *The Cinderella Cycle* and Warren

E. Roberts in *The Tale of the Kind and the Unkind Girls*. The heroes or heroines of such tales epitomize the eleventh commandment: "Thou shalt never give up." The contrasting personalities of children have fascinated the world from India and Japan to Europe and America. Minor motifs come and go, but the change of fortune between two characters who are kind and unkind, modest and conceited, or courteous and discourteous supplies a structure that is easy to tell and satisfying to hear. The summary dismissal of the "bad" sister at the end of the English variant has humorous overtones.

By contrast the Greek version told by Megas (*Greece*, Tale 39, "The Twelve Months," pp. 123–27) maintains seriousness throughout, and the structure is beautifully arranged around twelve young men representing the twelve months of the year, each with a gift for humanity. Each man gives the best of his month to the grateful mother of a large, poor family. The sharp contrast between the appreciative mother and the scornful mother who envies her makes an effective conclusion.

Three Japanese versions from Seki (*Japan*, Tales 33, 34, and 35), provide further examples. Tale 33 contains the nauseating test of drinking water in which cows, horses, and vegetables have been washed; only then can the husband find his pet sparrow whose tongue his cruel wife had cut. Tale 34 is constructed from the motif of being tormented by having to continually break wind (D2063.5). The lord of the region makes an old man repeat the stunt of pulling a bird's legs sticking from his anus to cause himself to break wind. The revenge in this tale is suffered by the greedy man who claims he too can break wind but only gets his buttocks cut when the angry lord sees what a failure he is. Tale 35 departs even further from the serious theme of kind and unkind people. An old man follows directions from his dog, who leads him to coins buried in a mountain; the dog continues to play benefactor for quite a while. A neighbor tries to do likewise, but fails to follow the dog's directions and receives only snakes, frogs, and centipedes. In disgust he kills the dog, but the dog's owner and his wife get more money from the ground when they dig the dog's grave. The tale continues with further good luck and bad luck, all of which is supposed to inculcate the moral of not trying to imitate other people.

A significant variant of Type 480 is "Tolerance and Jealousy" (Brenda E. F. Beck et al., *Folktales of India*, Tale 34, pp. 118–21). Rivalry among women often appears in stories from India. In the typical plot of "The Kind and the Unkind Girls," the two central characters are usually either sisters or daughter and stepdaughter. In this Indian tale from Tamilnadu, the jealous mother motivates her daughter to emulate the success of her stepdaughter, whose kindness has won her a prince in the opening episode; but the unkind daughter wins only a shepherd. This archetypal sequence of the kind girl being followed by the unkind one is reversed in the Florida story, which opens with the cruelty of one sister, surpassed by the tenderness of the other sister. In spite of this difference in narrative structure, both the Indian and Florida stories use moral tags as conclusions. Since, however, the final platitude is the only one among the ninety-nine tales in this collection from

India, it may reflect the European tendency to add trite morals to stories, as Perrault did in his French tales and as the Florida storyteller does in her closing admonition.

In Egypt *The Kind and the Unkind* is nearly always told by adult females and children. Among Egyptian tales it remains the most popular sort of *Märchen*, along with Type 511A, *The Little Red Ox*. Males tend to be less interested in this sort of individual rivalry because in Egypt they (unlike the females) leave home and enter larger social groups, so that their stories deal more with rivalry among males in war, adventures, and the like (El-Shamy, *Egypt,* "Introduction," pp. lii–liii.) It may be worth noting that the Florida tale was told by a black adult woman to a young white girl.

Type 620: The Presents

Motif Q2, *Kind and unkind,* has appeared in a variety of tales representing Types 431 and 480, as noted in the comments above. Whether the Florida tale of "Peazy and Beanzy" should also be seen as belonging to Type 620 depends on how one perceives its structure. The Florida tale ends with the presents awarded to the kind sister. Like the typical form noted by Thompson in *The Folktale* (p. 126) and in Aarne and Thompson's *Types of the Folktale* (p. 224), the Florida narrative starts with the haughty sister and her failures, followed by the successes of the helpful sister. The comparative scarcity of *The Presents* in world collections is worth noting. The known versions may be diminished versions of the longer tales that have faded from memory. This Florida tale is one of the liveliest.

13. The Milky Way

This account of the way to the sky came from Josie Billie, a Seminole Indian, who related it to Robert F. Greenlee in 1939. (See Greenlee's "Folktales of the Florida Seminole," 138–39.)

Type 471: The Bridge to the Other World

Among stories of extraordinary or superhuman tasks and their rewards, the Seminole Indian belief in good people, along with their dogs and horses, traveling across the Milky Way to the eternal world in the sky shows the intent of the great Breathmaker to prepare a place for spirits remaining faithful to him. Among the Seminoles life itself is the universal quest, without any fear of ghosts, since they believe spirits never return from the sky. The pattern of this story modifies the more typical human quest in the archetypal form of the tale, in which several brothers search for a lost sister and only the youngest brother listens to the advice of a bird that tells him to cross a bridge; those who fail to cross are turned to stone. The central motif of a bridge to the land of the dead (E481.2.1) is maintained in both versions.

Reidar Thorwald Christiansen's "The Seven Foals" (*Folktales of Norway,* Tale 71) uses the stock character of the youngest brother. Without the religious aura of many versions, the Norwegian tale treats the boys as lazy fools who always take the easiest way out, until the youngest (Ash Boy) resists the temptation of lingering with the old hag who has delayed the older brothers. Ash Boy cares for the foals that the others had neglected, and discovers that the horses are really brothers of a princess, whom he marries. The crossing of the bridge is only a minor incident along the way.

The tale has certain religious overtones; for example, the brothers in horse form are found to be human when they eat communion bread and wine. But the tale keeps its lighthearted atmosphere to the end, when the storyteller tells us that although he attended the wedding all he got was a piece of cake with butter on it; and when he put the slice on the stove, the cake burned and the butter ran so that he couldn't eat even a crumb.

14. Buried Treasure

Variant A

It is a moot point whether the motifs of such a story belong more to folktale or legend. True events often blend with folk imagination to make an effective account of what "really happened" in many Florida stories. Type 968, *Miscellaneous Robber and Murder Stories*, seems to be a proper category for this Wakulla account kept alive in local retelling.

In both life and literature, vice and virtue appear repeatedly in the same familiar guises, until reality appears to imitate fantasy. Florida crimes often involve the murder and easy burial of the victims in sand or swamps. Corpses frequently turn up in boxes or holes; skeletons of missing people come to light in fields and forests, as they do in folktales.

The Wakulla event was reported to me by Mrs. Alvidra F. Johnston (born in 1914), who lived in various parts of Wakulla County as well as in Tallahassee. A fine school teacher who attended the Florida State University in the 1930s and the 1950s, she was a kind of encyclopedia of North Florida lore.

Mrs. Johnston knew Mr. J. E. Stansbury when he was quite old, probably in his seventies. While he was acting as subsecretary of agriculture in Havana, Cuba, he found there several records of ships sunk along the Florida coast, and maps where treasure was supposed to be buried. At the end of World War I, he bought a boat in New Orleans to sail to New York. While passing Ochlockonee Bay, he thought he recognized a mound as the one he had studied on a chart. He anchored nearby at Sopchoppy and completed his trip to New York by train. Returning with maps, he found a house for his wife and four children, who moved to Wakulla County in 1922. Although he was well informed about treasures in the local counties, he never found any. While he was living along the Sopchoppy River, he said, treasure turned up in ten of the twelve sites indicated in the twelve maps he had brought with him. He maintained that the treasures were found by a Wakulla County man and a Tallahassean, who kept their discovery quiet to avoid taxes.

According to Mr. Stansbury and his friend Joe Nichols, the most valuable treasure lies buried in quicksand. It is located near the mouth of the Ochlockonee River, where a large white shell mound adjacent to the site can be seen from the bridge over the Ochlockonee Bay. Directly west of the bridge, it is the highest elevation in the vicinity.

With Mr. G. S. Johnston, Jr., a Tallahassee attorney and Alvidra's husband, they supervised the convicts hired for the state to dig out the gold in the late twenties and early thirties. Mr. Nichols said that "a little ways underground we found this skeleton—just the whole man. Lawyer Johnston's boy and Mr. Stansbury's two younguns, they took it, but I don't know what they done with it." (Alvidra Johnston said they put it in a boat, rowed over to Old Fields, and left it in the house of a man they disliked.)

Mrs. Johnston said that a diviner with a hickory limb and another with a metal-locating contraption insisted that gold is still down there, but that each time more digging was done, air hitting the chest caused it to sink deeper. Grappling hooks once tore a piece of copper-bound mahogany from the chest. People think that the chest now rests on solid limestone. (After several years the St. Joe Paper Company took over the property and forbade any further digging.)

The Wakulla story reflects well-known motifs: N511 (*Treasure in ground*), N525 (*Treasure found in chest [kettle, cask]*), and D1712 (*Soothsayer [diviner, oracle, etc.]*).

Variant B

This Wacissa version came from Eugene Nabi, who heard it from Walter Cornelius Teate, Sr., in 1952. Mr. Teate was born near Wacissa in 1886. Mr. Nabi, who lived in Jacksonville, where he was born in 1931, adopted the Gulf Coast town of Wacissa as his favorite representative of the Florida rural life.

15. Dividing the Crops

This tale came from Mose Miles, several of whose stories appeared above in Animal Tales, beginning with Tale 1.

Type 1030: The Crop Division

Such a tale depends on the folk belief in the clear-cut division between good and evil. God and devil, man and monster, fox and bear exercise their right to divide the world. The Florida variant uses the fox and the rabbit in a comic episode between traditional rivals dividing the fruits of the harvest. Usually in this kind of tale the smarter character is playing a trick based on his greater knowledge about the crops. But here the rabbit promises all the underground crops to the fox, who appears unusually stupid since peanuts as well as potatoes must be harvested from roots below ground. Thus in this story the deception is not based on knowledge of what crops grow above or below the ground, but is simply a matter of the rabbit stealing from the fox.

Deceptive bargains occur in the Chinese tale "The Living King of

Hell Dies in Anger" (Eberhard, *China*, Tale 70, pp. 179–80). In this story the landlord exploited the farmers so much they called him the Living King of Hell. At first the landlord was tricked out of his bargain to take the "upper half" of the crops because the farmer planted only taro, a root crop. Reversing the agreement, the landlord was again cheated out of his harvest because the next year the farmer grew only wheat. Thinking at last to defeat the tricky farmer, the landlord said he would take the top and bottom ends of the harvest while the farmer would get only the middle. Yet the farmer still outwitted the landlord by planting popcorn, which had nothing of value on either end of its stalks; and the landlord died of sleepless nights caused by his anger.

Eberhard observes that this tale is the only one of its type from China known to him, although he recognizes it has wide distribution in Asia and Europe (p. 238). The cheating of the upper class may result from the Communist system in China, Eberhard suggests.

God and the devil set out to sow wheat at the very beginning of the world's cultivation in a French tale from Lower Marche (Massignon, *France*, pp. 121–22). Although to all appearances the devil seems stronger than God, he knows nothing about edible plants, so God gets the grain, the potatoes, and the maize in a series of tricks similar to those in the Chinese tale: crops aboveground, underground, or both. But the devil is still too stupid to learn from his experiences with God: he exchanges his stone castle for God's ice castle, which God then melts in the sun.

All such tales develop in local ways Motif K171.1, *Deceptive crop division: above the ground, below the ground.*

This motif has appeared in Egypt in several variants but not in sub-Saharan Africa, although other kinds of deceptive divisions appear in African collections (El-Shamy, *Egypt*, p. 291). In eastern African groups Type 1030 is followed by Type 1074, *Race Won by Deception: Relative Helpers* (El-Shamy, p. 292).

16. Chopping Off a Head

This kind of tale was known to several of Virginia Spencer's black friends in Leon County. Her version follows the manner of swapping stories practiced by Ben Fields and Samuel Sampson (see notes for Tales 4 and 5).

Type 1065*: Contest in Chopping

Contests and races still form a suspenseful part of storytelling. Traditionally there is a kind of folk Olympiad of events to show strength and skill. The participants may be people or animals from all countries of the world. Sometimes deception and even cruelty triumph over fairness in these contests.

In the Leon County cycles of animal tales, the cruelty of the chopping contest, in which Rooster tricks Rabbit into having his head chopped off, seems shocking. Even worse, Rabbit's own wife is happy about his death.

In this version the basic motif is E783, *Vital head.*

17. The Vengeful Corpse

This tragicomic tale was told to me by Marie Enno, born in Key West, Florida, in 1929. I knew her from 1949 to 1951, when she had a wide acquaintance with the lore of Tampa.

One of the most elaborate literary offerings about the revenge of the dead is "Imprisoned with the Pharoahs," by H. P. Lovecraft (*The Doom That Came to Sarnath*, pp. 176–205). While Lovecraft dismissed the episode as a dream, the folktale makes it a reality.

Type 1699*: The Coffin-Maker

This type of tale involves Motif X422, *The corpse with his feet cut off.* In the standard AT Type 1699* there is a practical motivation: the coffin was made too short, so the corpse's feet must be cut off so that the body can fit into it. The Florida tale becomes a horror story because the coffin-maker switched coffins to make it possible for the poor dead man whom everyone liked to be buried in the finer coffin of the despised rich man. The gashes inflicted on the coffin-maker's legs when his feet fall into this coffin are an alternate ending to Type 1699*, which closes with the ironic remark of the priest at the funeral of the footless corpse: "On the last day he will rise."

A related motif is S162, *Mutilation: cutting off legs (feet).*

18. The Lucky Shot

In the 1950s Sara Jane Pilcher introduced me to some of her friends in Okaloosa County in and around Laurel Hill. Among them was Mack Tyner, who, Sara Jane said, always believed a good laugh was better than a doctor. Mr. Tyner claimed he was the biggest liar in the wiregrass and gallberry country, still young in his eighties. On the serious side, he tried to advance the welfare of his county, the Masonic Order, and the Republican party.

This hunting tale came from Mr. Tyner.

Type 1890: The Lucky Shot

Dorson mentions this story, America's favorite tall tale, in *American Folklore* (p. 45). From a closer study of its variants, I have shown that Type 1890 (Motif X1110) frequently combines with other motifs to create various structures found in the stories of several southern states (see my "From Reality to Fantasy: Opening-Closing Formulas in the Structures of American Tall Tales").

19. The Continual Liar

This kind of tale represents the epitome of tall tales and exaggerations, the effect of such stretchers depending on whether the listener accepts the event as fact or fiction, "history" or "legend."

This version came to me from Martha Spencer of Laurel Hill, Florida, where I visited her and her family in 1953. Several family members were good tellers of tales, ballad singers, and carriers of beliefs and customs.

Type 1920B: The One Says, "I Have Not Time to Lie" and Yet Lies

More a joke than a fully developed tale, this type usually shows how the liar can fool some people into not knowing he is still lying. Dorson mentions this kind of incident in *American Folklore* (pp. 132, 229) as part of the continuing cycle of anecdotes from successful liars who don't know when to stop lying. Gib Morgan is probably the most famous folk hero of this kind; his yarns were widely spread through the oil fields in Ohio, West Virginia, and Pennsylvania.

20. *The Land of the Lazy*

This tale appeals to the side of human nature that wants something for little or nothing. The French of the Middle Ages knew this land of comfort without work as Cockaigne; the Germans called it Schlaraffenland. It is in the tradition of the Promised Land of the Hebrews, a land of milk and honey. The Florida version is the land of "Diddy-Wah-Diddy," a kind of heaven for black people, where there is always good food to eat, with curbstones as comfortable as sitting chairs on which you can sit and survey the baked chicken, sweet potato pie, and other delectable food, which never runs out; the more you eat, the faster it grows. (See Zora Neale Hurston, Federal Writers' Project manuscripts, pp. 40–45.) Comparable paradises can be found in the Grimms' Tale 158, "The Story of Schlaraffenland," and Tale 159, "The Ditmars Tale of Wonders."

This North Florida account came from George Milton, born in 1918 in Marianna, Florida. He heard the stories from his mother, Mrs. Myrtle Merritt Wilson, a Marianna native, who got them from a black woman known as Aunt Rachel, only in her teens when the incidents were said to have occurred.

Type 1930: Schlaraffenland

The will to believe in distant happy places persists in life and lore, especially when they are so far from earth that things impossible in this world can easily happen.

The "Land of the Idle" is the subject of chapter 17 in the story of Baron Munchausen's trip to the moon, where he was driven by a whirlwind and where he found inhabitants with three heads riding on huge griffins, flies as large as sheep, and spikes of horseradish or asparagus used as javelins and mushrooms as shields in the moon's war against the sun (R. E. Raspe et al., *The Adventures of Baron Munchausen*).

Fabulous exaggerations about the fertile lands of America became the subjects of folksongs known to Norwegians, Swedes, and Danes, and had even been kept alive in an Irish tale that Dorson heard in 1951 (*American Folklore*, pp. 150–52).

Pino-Saavedra (*Chile*, Tale 49) presents an elaborate combination of Schlaraffenland settings with other lies and exaggerations from Chilean swindlers, who try to fool kings or emperors in Chile, Spain, and France with stories about the plains of Africa, where a cabbage plant is so large it holds an entire Chilean squadron on one leaf. The huge cabbage is of course cooked in a huge pot (Types 1960D, *The Great Vegetable*, and 1960F, *The Great Kettle*).

Type 1930 occurs as a separate story throughout the Middle East, where it usually involves a lying contest, as well as in sub-Saharan Africa. El-Shamy's longer narrative (*Egypt*, Tale 3) starts with Type 465, *The Man Persecuted because of His Beautiful Wife*, followed by Type 1930. Although the tale is popular in Egypt, there are numerous variations on the elements of the beginning episode, where the supernatural beautiful wife may be missing, with attention given to parts 2 and 2a of Type 465, involving difficult quests or tasks (see *Egypt*, p. 244).

In *American Folklore* (p. 52) Dorson says, "The mythical land of Cockaigne, a fairy-tale glutton's paradise, is grafted onto the Great West, where pigs' tails planted in the rich bottom lands produce a crop of young porkers, pieces of steel sprout into jackknives, and even the deer obligingly carry a bucket of salt on their rumps and turn them to the squatter's fire until their hind parts are juicily cooked."

21. Larger than Life

These anecdotes turned up in conversations with Mack Tyner of Laurel Hill (see note for Tale 18).

The sequence of anecdotes depends on Motif K1888 (*Illusory light*), X1154 (*Lie: unusual catch by fisherman*), and X1301 (*Lie: the great fish*).

The people swapping stories have a clear mutual appreciation for the artistic heights of fancy that may be achieved with the tall tale.

Type 1960B: The Great Fish

Fishermen always like to brag about the size of the fish they've caught; such exaggerations among fishermen and hunters spontaneously happen around the world. Here the fish story is coupled with a fisherman exaggeration about a lantern, still burning underwater six years after he had kicked it into the river (Motif 1154). A similar sequence of tall tales appears in the story of a Turkish soldier returning home, including the great vegetable (Type 1960D) and the great kettle (Type 1960F). (See Warren S. Walker and Ahmet E. Uysal, *Tales Alive in Turkey*, Tale 13, pt. 3, pp. 165–71.)

22. Origin of Seminole Clans and Black People

These origin stories were told in 1939 by Josie Billie to Robert F. Greenlee, who reported them in "Folktales of the Florida Seminole," p. 141. Josie Billie acted as an intermediary between tribesmen and

Greenlee, a white man the Seminoles were reluctant to take into their confidence.

The central element in both versions is Motif A875.1, *Navel of the earth*. Both are "emergence myths," with human beings springing forth from Mother Earth, who gives birth from a mountain—difficult in Florida, which has no mountains.

The obvious blend of Indian and Christian lore appears in Variant B with the early arrival of Jesus to launch the birth of the clans.

Aside from the typical identification of each clan with an aspect of nature representing a particular power, a close social proximity in early generations is reflected in Variant A between Indians and black people in Florida, since blacks appear last in the birth sequence.

Another version of how black people became black, from Eatonville, Florida, was repeated by Zora Neale Hurston in *Mules and Men*. Some people were loafing behind on the day God gave out color. When the angels "Rayfield" and "Gab'ull" found them, they pushed and shoved until they nearly upset God's throne. "So God hollered 'Git back! Git back!' and they misunderstood him and thought he said, 'Git black,' and they been black ever since" (*Mules and Men*, p. 49).

Less reliable origins for Florida and its Spanish moss appear in the literary retelling of Marion E. Gridley's *Indian Legends of American Scenes* (Chicago and New York: M. A. Donohue, 1939). The account of Florida's origin in Gridley uses Motif A15.2, *Brothers as creators*.

23. The Flood

This version of the universal flood also came from Josie Billie (see preceding note) and includes Motifs A1010 (*Deluge*), A1021 (*Deluge: escape in boat [ark]*), and A1022 (*Escape from deluge on mountain*).

This blend of the biblical story and Seminole belief fails to give any motivation for the flood. The big hill at the end is a better adaptation to the Florida landscape than the mountain origins in Tale 22. These hilly settings may be the result of memories of Georgia mountains from ancestors who invented the tales, or perhaps the influence of the Bible stories. Even "big hills" occur mainly in northern Florida, and they are not very large.

Only the animals and the Indians know the meaning of the green sprigs that the birds carry since they are closer to nature than other beings.

Another adaptation of the flood story to Florida is an account still mentioned here and there in oral anecdotes about North Florida, based on the speculations of E. E. Callaway of Bristol. He published a pamphlet (undated, but probably in the 1940s) in which he concludes that the original Garden of Eden was located near Bristol because the river system in this part of the state resembles the description in the second chapter of Genesis.

After the Flood the names of these rivers, as well as those of the lands around them (Euphrates, Ethiopia, Syria, etc.), were transferred to Asia and Africa; later the rivers were renamed (Chattahoochee, Flint, etc.).

Another telling point in the oral legends is the fact that gopher wood, from which Noah's Ark was made, grows nowhere on earth except between Bristol and Chattahoochee, Florida. God's command in Genesis 6: 14 to build the Ark of gopher wood, covered with pitch inside and outside, was obeyed nine miles north of Bristol. After it was loaded with animals and people, the Ark floated on the deep flood waters, aided by winds, from Bristol to Mt. Ararat. In the limestone of the Florida countryside the bones can be found from every animal that ever lived on earth. The Apalachicola Valley of Florida, then, is the site of the original Garden of Eden.

24. The Giants of Florida

Variant A

This tale involving the "Giant sickness" came from the Seminole Josie Billie, who said that the medicine to cure this sickness was blown through ancient bamboo pipes (see Greenlee, "Folktales of the Florida Seminole," p. 140).

The central motif is A1301, *Man at first as large as giants*.

Variant B

This legend, locally famous around Carrabelle, Florida, came from J. Edward Bell, Jr., in the summer of 1958. He had heard it as it circulated among members of the Crum family living in Carrabelle and vicinity, a huge family, said Bell, "of great fishers and talkers." Typical motifs are A1301 (*Man at first as large as giants*), A1315.1 (*Why man became gray-headed*), A1315.2 (*Origin of bald heads*), A1331 (*Paradise lost*), F531.0.4 (*Giant woman*), and F531.1.6.3.2 (*Giant without hair*). These motifs form one of Florida's most enduring stories of "departure and return."

25. Origin of Spanish Moss

Born in Miami, Florida, in 1938, Gloria R. King told me this story in 1958, when she was living in Coral Gables. She had heard it from James McFaggart of Bonifay.

Less romanticized than the postcard versions sold to tourists, this legend involves such motifs as D213.4.1* (*Transformation: man to Spanish moss*) and F545.1 (*Remarkable beard*).

26. Origins of Seminole Indian Food

The informant was Josie Billie, quoted by Greenlee ("Folktales of the Florida Seminole," pp. 138, 141). The story includes Motifs A185.7 (*God prepares food for mortal*), A1423 (*Acquisition of vegetables and* cereals), A2600 (*Origin of plants*), and A2611.0.5 (*Parts of human or animal body transformed into plants*).

The combination of the corn people and Jesus reflects the Christianizing of Seminole belief. Jesus' pocket full of turkey feathers and his divine assistance in helping catch turkeys is an amusing, vivid detail. In general Jesus plays the role of a god of agriculture in Seminole lore (Motif A541.2). In another account Jesus, after traveling from Georgia to Miami, gave the Indians some little cakes which covered the ground and, after a rain, sprouted roots, from which grew the koonti plant ("Folktales of the Florida Seminole," p. 138).

27. Origin of Hushpuppies

At Lake Iamonia, Florida, I learned this version of the beginning of this dish from our cook, Aunt Rachel, an aged black woman who claimed to have lived in Civil War days. She told me her story in 1948. According to her, she had been cooking at fish fries for more than thirty years before she had her dream.

Her vocabulary was especially interesting because she used *stakle* for dream and *p'noblums* for hushpuppies. The closest word to *p'noblums* I have been able to find is *monobilies*, a word used among some rural people in South Georgia for hushpuppies.

Chief motifs are A1420.2 (*Gods teach how to seek and prepare food*) and A1420.3 (*Creator of food items*).

The "divine" origin of something dear to its owner has an interesting Florida analogy in Alton Morris's account of "The Cherry Tree Carol" (Child Ballad 54), inspired by a dream of Mrs. G. A. Griffin of Newberry, Florida. She told him that she valued this song, which she called "Sweet Mary and Sweet Joseph," because it was the only one she had created herself. Mrs. Griffin visited a folklore class studying American balladry at the University of Florida in Gainesville during the summer of 1940, and sang her version of this ballad. She insisted she had never heard it anywhere before the afternoon of her inspiration. (See Morris, *Folksongs of Florida*, p. 262.)

28. Origin of Packenham's Rum (The Corpse in the Cask)

Helen Weaver of Tallahassee, whom I knew in the 1950s, liked to tell this tale from her father. It includes Motifs A1427.3* (*Origin of rum [Packenham's]*), C624.1* (*Forbidden barrel of rum contains corpse*), and S160.6* (*Corpse mutilated by cutting off its head*).

The continuing interest in this kind of legend is documented in Jan Harold Brunvand's *The Choking Doberman and Other "New" Urban Legends* (pp. 115–16). Brunvand recounts the story circulated about the British naval hero Admiral Horatio Nelson, whose body was preserved in a cask of brandy (not rum, as some tales say). He also mentions General Edward Pakenham [*sic*], the hero of the Battle of New Orleans in 1815, whose remains were kept in wine (not rum). The wine barrel is said to have been accidentally shipped to South Carolina, where the wine was served to party guests.

29. Early St. Augustine

This historic city, with its charming sixteenth-century Spanish architecture and colorful tropical vegetation, is the oldest permanent European settlement in the United States. Many of its tales and legends are kept alive by the family of E. L. Reyes, who told me in 1950 the anecdotes in my "Legends of the King's Highway."

The Reyes family belongs to a part of the St. Augustine population descended from the emigrés who came from the Mediterranean island of Minorca in 1767, when Dr. Andrew Turnbull tried to establish a Florida colony at New Smyrna. Among the first group of colonists were Greeks and Italians. They endured much suffering from harsh overseers until finally the settlers, repudiating their contracts, left New Smyrna for St. Augustine.

The St. Augustine stories in this volume also came from my visit with Mr. and Mrs. Reyes in 1950. Motifs, as they occur in order, are M341.2.0.1 (*Prophecy: death by particular weapon*), V253 (*Faithfulness to Virgin Mary, even if not to Christ, rewarded*), V254.2 (*Ship in storm saved because of sailors' "Ave Maria"*), V115.4.1* (*Agony bell rung to announce death*), J1705.5* (*Stupid engineer*), Q411 (*Death as punishment*), Q413.0.1 (*Threat of hanging*), M110 (*Taking of vows and oaths*), P711 (*Patriotism*), and F548.0.2* (*Short legs*).

30. José Gaspar

Alice Welch was born in 1927 and lived most of her early life in Tampa, Florida. I collected this account from her in 1948.

Central motifs in the Gaspar legend are E422.1.10 (*Dismembered corpse*), J216.7* (*Pirate prefers drowning himself to being captured*), N511.1 (*Treasure buried by men*), P170 (*Slaves*), R12.5* (*Ship captured by meeting of pirates*), and S133 (*Murder by beheading*).

Numerous pirate legends are associated with the long coastlines of Florida. In the summer of 1949, in Key West, E. A. Strunk reminded me that after pirates were put out of business by the fast schooners, they made deals with the Key West lighthouse keeper to put out the light and let them use the lights on their pirate ships to mislead boats offshore. Sometimes pirates made a deal with a ship's captain to wreck his own ship and then split the booty fifty-fifty with the pirates.

This last practice inspired a famous Key West story, known in several versions to Mr. Strunk, which I summarize: A man sitting in church near a window to the sea sees a ship about to be wrecked. He runs from the church to be the first one there, and others follow to race him to the shore, breaking up the church service. In some versions the minister himself, from his high place in the pulpit, is the first to see that a ship has gone aground off a reef. He asks all the members of the congregation to bow their heads for a long prayer. While their heads are bowed, the minister walks down the aisle and leaves the church so that he can be the first one out to the wreck. In 1985, in Ft. Lauderdale, I heard the same anecdote from Russell Cleaver Stevralia of Key West, who told me the legend still flourishes there.

The story features Motifs F931.5.1* (*Shipwreck caused by misleading lights*) and W151.11* (*Greedy preacher has congregation bow heads so that he can be the first to reach spoils of shipwreck outside church*).

31. The Dark Nights in May

This Indian legend about the Manatee River came from Thomas M. Looney, a resident of Tampa, Florida, where he was born in 1925. I recorded it in 1949, as he recounted it in his dramatic, almost oratorical style of speaking. It has Motifs D1233 (*Magic violin [fiddle]*) and E425.1.1 (*Revenant as lady in white*).

32. The She-Man

This legend was told to me by Peter M. Findley in the summer of 1949. He was born in Brighton, England, in 1927, and spent his later life in Orlando, Florida. He told me that many people residing near the river vow that the story is true. Its motifs are K1813.3* (*Man disguises himself as his wife after her murder*), N511.1 (*Treasure buried by men*), S123 (*Buried alive*), T24.3 (*Madness from love*), and T211.5 (*Man becomes a hermit after his wife's death*).

33. Choosing the Site for the State Capitol

This version from Inez Walker of Wakulla County as she told it in the summer of 1949 differs considerably from historical records. Her legend is a fine example of how people like to embroider their past to make it better than it really was.

The historical account as given by Bertram H. Groene in *Ante-Bellum Tallahassee* (pp. 14–16) was anything but an easy trip to a pleasant midpoint between St. Augustine and Pensacola. Dr. William H. Simmons of St. Augustine and John Lee Williams of Pensacola, the commissioners for Governor DuVal, suffered many hardships and delays while they tried to find each other in the wilderness, and then argued at length about the location.

While Simmons rode from St. Augustine on horseback, Williams made a sea voyage from Pensacola to St. Marks, the agreed-upon meeting place. He did not meet Simmons on time at St. Marks because a storm sank his boat at St. George Island, where his company survived on oysters and crabs after their food supply ran out. Disgusted with the boat's captain, Williams set out on his own to try to cross the land on foot. He wandered for five days on St. James Island, managed to cross the Ochlockonee River on a makeshift raft, and finally met the boat waiting for him along the shore. Exhausted from hunger, thirst, and fatigue, he arrived at St. Marks.

But even when Simmons and Williams reached the small waterfall later known to Tallahasseans as the Cascade, their problems were not over. Williams loved the beauty of the forests and hills but Simmons held out for a location farther to the east, since he represented St.

Augustine interests. He insisted that a location near the mouth of the Suwannee River would be a preferable place. But when they tried to investigate it, they could not even find the broad mouth of the river. Only after Simmons's patience was worn out did he give in to Williams's original choice of the Cascade as the capitol site.

Motifs are F700 (*Extraordinary places*) and F141.5* (*Waterfall as location for state capitol*).

34. Legendary Tallahassee

Born in 1912 and a resident of Orlando, Florida, for several years, Wilda Larson lived in Tallahassee during the 1940s and 1950s, where she heard many legends of the city and taught English classes in Tallahassee public schools.

Miss Larson came to appreciate the local lore of Tallahassee and felt that it had been neglected. She had collected stories from several friends, whom she wished to acknowledge: Nan Page of Woodville, who had lived near Tallahassee all her life; William Cash, the state librarian, who had moved to Tallahassee in 1925; B. W. Partridge, B. Whitfield, and Mary Davis, descendant of the Demilly family, all lifetime residents of Tallahassee; and Mary Gay, an elderly black woman who had worked at the Biddle plantation.

Miss Larson was proud to relate these episodes to me, for she felt they gave a better idea of early Tallahassee life than any official history. In her retelling of them, she made them her own.

Motifs that appear in the stories are:

a. "Aunt Memory": D799.4* (*Disenchantment by sweeping disturbed ground*), D1040 (*Magic drink*).

b. "Tiger Tail": P310.10* (*Indian friend guards white children*).

c. "The Osceola Oak Tree": D1483.3.1* (*Magic tree: when planted, will never die*), D1487.3.1* (*Tree magically protected against all efforts to kill it*), K354.2* (*Trickster feigns hospitality but kills guests and takes their money*).

d. "Lake Legends": F713.2 (*Bottomless lakes [pools, etc.]*), F718.13* (*Spring originates from spot where vanished lovers stood*), F725.10* (*Stone with Andrew Jackson's name at bottom of lake*).

e. "The Cherokee Rose": H602.3.1* (*Cherokee Rose symbolizes loss of Indian girl belonging to the Cherokee tribe*).

f. "Spanish Treasure": N517.2 (*Treasure hidden within wall [under floor] of house*).

g. "The Goodwood Plantation": P201.2* (*Feud between neighboring families*).

h. "The Smoky Swamp": A2816 (*Origin of smoke*), D1812.5.0.4 (*Rising smoke as omen*).

i. "Prince Murat": F929.2.2* (*Dinner guests swallow buzzard meat unwittingly*).

j. "Mrs. Lewis Lively": M451.1 (*Death by suicide*).

k. "The Lafayette Tree": E422.1.11.4 (*Revenant as skeleton*).

l. "Old Man Eppes": E332 (*Nonmalevolent road ghosts*), E334.1 (*Ghost haunts scene of former misfortune or crime*).

m. "The White Goat": E521.6* (*Ghost as white goat*).

n. "The Soft-Shelled Turtle": E525* (*Ghost as turtle, becomes smaller until it disappears*).

o. "The Lop-Eared Dog": E521.2.3* (*Ghostly dog grows larger, but one ear stays small*).

p. "The Vision": E332.3.3.2* (*Vanishing visitor, disappears walking backwards*).

q. "Night Watch": E539.1.2* (*Bolted door blows open*).

r. "A Snake Attack": B754.7.3* (*Snake's offspring born through mouth*).

s. "The St. Marks Cow": F715.3 (*Rivers with marvelous underground connections*), F949.1 (*Animal sinks into earth*), R211.3 (*Escape through underground passage*), and X1545 (*Lies about remarkable underground channels*).

t. "Rain": X1153 (*Lie: fish caught by remarkable trick*).

u. "Cows on the Road": J2341.1* (*Near-sighted man thinks cows on road are spots on windshield*).

v. "The Tallahassee Train": J1649.1* (*Mistaken act: engineer congratulated on having train arrive on time says: "But this is yesterday's train!"*) and X1815.2 (*Lies about slow trains*).

35. Lost at Sea

This story is kept alive mainly by the monuments standing in front of old St. John's Episcopal Church on Monroe Street in Tallahassee. While it echoes Tale 34g, the two accounts are told separately from each other, one to explain the ownership of the Goodwood Plantation, the other to explain why there are two monuments in front of the church.

This version was told to me by Mildred Winfield (originally from Ocala, Florida), while she was living in Tallahassee in 1950. It includes Motifs N300 (*Unlucky accidents*) and P201.2* (*Feud between neighboring families*). It is a good example of how history becomes reworked in popular memories. The facts of the case concerning the Croom (not Broom) family are in Bertram Groene's *Ante-Bellum Tallahassee* (p. 46) and are more fully described in Gloria Jahoda's *The Other Florida* (pp. 76–80). The Croom family traveled by steamship from New York to Charleston, South Carolina; the party consisted of Mr. and Mrs. Hardy Croom, a Mrs. Camack (an aunt of Mrs. Croom's), and the three Croom children, Henrietta, William, and Justina. The court case after the drownings established that the son, William, was the last one to die in the storm, according to the testimony of survivors. The trip was not a honeymoon, and only one of the two monuments in front of the Episcopal church is dedicated to the Croom family.

36. Tallahassee Houses

Born in Jacksonville, Florida, in 1929, Newell Martin was living in Tallahassee when he told me these legends in 1949. They contain the following motifs: The Flagg House—F952.8* (*Blindness cured by stroke of lightning*), N6 (*Luck in gambling*), and X1710 (*Lies about numbers*); The Columns—N517.2 (*Treasure hidden within wall [under floor] of house*).

37. The Last Tallahassee Indians

This legend also came from Newell Martin in 1949. Its central motif is N619* (*Child falling accidentally scares Indians*).

38. Wakulla Pocahontas

Wakulla County, south of Leon County with its capital city Tallahassee, still has many of its native forests, wildlife, springs, and streams. It is also the scene of the Florida Pocahontas story told to me by Inez Walker, a county resident in 1949.

According to W. T. Cash, state librarian, this event occurred in 1818 and the soldier's name was Duncan McCrimmon. Mr. Cash added that the chief compensated the Indians for their disappointment at sparing the soldier by promising them the opportunity to sample some of the liquor if they were chosen as guards to accompany the soldier. Mr. Cash provided a sequel unhappy for the father but happy for the daughter. As he heard the story, less than three months later, when General Andrew Jackson came to fight the Florida Indians, he captured and hanged Prophet Francis; but Duncan married Malee and they moved across the Suwannee River into present-day Alachua County, where they lived happily for many years.

The central motif of this story is K512.5* (*Compassionate executioner: obtaining liquor in place of burning prisoner at stake*).

39. Chief Tom Tiger

This story is from Betty Woodall's grandmother in Kissimmee (see note for Tale 44). Although Betty found that her grandmother's recollections varied from accounts of the Seminoles as given in Minnie Moore Willson's *History of Osceola County: Florida Frontier Life* as well as in Willson's *The Seminoles of Florida*, she realized that her grandmother's view was that of an outsider. She knew about the death of Chief Tom Tiger only as the Indians chose to tell of it, since he had died in the vastness of the Everglades. An unconnected set of events may have been gradually combined in her grandmother's memory; or perhaps she joined different occurrences to make a better story.

The story includes Motifs C602* (*Pact with snakes that if snakes never bite Seminole Indians they will never kill snakes*) and D1515.4.2 (*Snake stone applied to snakebite absorbs poison*).

40. The Skeleton in the Tree

Among the many mysterious disappearances and unexplained deaths in Florida, the legend of Horseshoe Plantation still lingers in people's memories. The plantation gained much popular attention when it was visited a few times by the duke and duchess of Windsor, who enjoyed hunting wild game in Florida. Esther C. Maglathin told this story to me in 1952, as she had heard it from Dr. A. R. Seymour, who heard it from Lucy Lester, professor of modern languages at the Florida State University. The Mr. Lester in the story was Miss Lester's father. Its climax depends on Motif Q491.1.3*, *Young man buried in tree after he is murdered to prevent his marriage.*

41. The Runaway Slave

Born in 1924, Helen Atwater of Chattahoochee, Florida, recalled this family legend in the spring of 1949. It includes Motifs H12 (*Recognition by song [music]*) and J710 (*Forethought in provision of food*).

42. Blood on the Floor

Gordon Louis Tillery was enthusiastic about the local lore of Winter Haven, Florida, where he was born in 1934. His father, William S. Tillery, had taken pride in telling him and his sisters about their family when they were youngsters. Louis told me this family story in the summer of 1955. It has Motifs D1654.3 (*Indelible blood*) and S139.4 (*Murder by mangling with axe*).

43. Capture by the "Enemy"

Thomas M. Looney, who had a penchant for telling romantic stories (see "The Dark Nights of May"), loved ghostly legends, especially those connected with his family. He said he had heard this story over and over in many ways from members of various branches of his family, who evidently liked florid rhetoric. He told it as he believed it had happened.

The young bugler in the story was his father's father. As it turned out, soon after he rejoined the Confederate army lines, the Civil War ended. But, Tom said, although his grandfather returned home as one of the vanquished, he was yet the victor.

The story includes Motifs D1960.4 (*Deathlike sleep*) and E125.4* (*Resuscitation by uncle*).

44. The Headless Horseman

Several family legends about Osceola County were told to me by Betty Woodall during the 1950s. She realized that much of this lore was not native to Kissimmee, her hometown, but had been brought to Florida by family members who were originally from Georgia.

Betty's paternal grandmother told her about the headless horseman, whose story she and other old-timers swore was true. Many of them said they had seen the headless horseman looking for his head at midnight near Canoe Creek. Betty said that maybe the horseman had found his head, because whenever she went camping in the vicinity of Deadman's Oak at midnight there was no horseman to be seen.

The story is an example of Motif E422.1.1 (*Headless revenant*).

45. The Haunted Kissimmee River

This story came from the family of Betty Woodall in Kissimmee. Betty remembered her father telling about this mysterious animal many times. Several motifs are used: E421 (*Spectral ghosts*), J1782.3.1* (*Noise in woods thought to be ghost*), K1725.2.1* (*Hunter thinks churning water is thrashing monster*), and E422.1.6.2.1* (*Revenant with only stumps for legs*).

46. Uncle Ben Yates

This story is from Elizabeth Vaviloff, who grew up in central Florida during the 1940s and 1950s. Its motif is J1149.13* (*Sheriff stays away from courthouse so that he cannot detect arsonist*).

47. Arcadia Heroes

This story came from Sara Crittenden, who had many friends in Arcadia, Florida, although she was born in Nova, Ohio, in 1917, and later lived in Willard, Ohio. She told me these legends in the fall of 1950.

a. "Acrefoot Johnson": Motifs F551.6* (*Remarkably enormous feet*), F681 (*Marvelous runner*).

b. "Ziba King": F513.1.2.2* (*Person with diamond-filled teeth*), F628.1.2.3* (*Man kills wild steer with one blow*), F632 (*Mighty eater*), N6.4* (*Man never beaten at stud poker*), V400 (*Charity*).

c. "Bone Mizelle": F543.1.3 (*Remarkably long, hooked nose*), J1325* (*Drunk man is not any Biblical character except Saul, who found his father's asses*), K1854.2* (*Corpse substituted for another so that it can go on a trip it had always wanted to take*), P673.1* (*Footwashing for burial should not be allowed because man would not let anybody wash his feet when he was alive*), X136* (*Humor of lisping*), X811.1* (*Drunk man wakes up in cemetery and thinks he is first one up on Judgment Day*).

d. "W. F. Espenlaub": B765.14.2* (*Man overcomes snake's hypnotic stare by waving gun at snake*).

e. "McClellan: W111.1.7* (*Man so lazy he would rather be buried alive than dig potatoes for himself*).

48. Wacissa Folks

These memories of Wacissa, Florida, were told to me in 1952 by Eugene Nabi (born in Jacksonville in 1931); he had heard them from Wacissa residents.

Central motifs are E425.2 (*Revenant as man*), E421.3 (*Luminous ghosts*), D1162 (*Magic light*), D1322.2 (*Light moving toward cemetery as sign of death*), E425.1.1 (*Revenant as lady in white*), E248* (*Ghosts stop car motor so that car can't enter cemetery*), X972 (*Lie: remarkable fighter*), X955 (*Lie: Remarkable killer*), X942 (*Lie: remarkable carrier*), X932 (*Lie: remarkable drinker*), S183 (*Frightful meal*), D1654.3 (*Indelible blood*), M398 (*Futility of weather prophecies*).

49. Cursed Clock

This well-known Marianna legend came from Zelma Hicks in 1949. She had lived all her life in Marianna. Its central motif is H252.7* (*Cursed courthouse clock never runs correctly*).

50. Family Friends

As noted earlier, Barbara Hudnall lived in Marianna, Florida, during her early life, although she was born at Birmingham in 1929. These family stories, which Barbara told me in 1949, may be characterized as memorates, personal narratives, but some of them appeared to be developing into local legends because they were familiar to other Marianna residents.

Central motifs in the order in which they occur in Barbara's account are: T596.3* (*Girl named Virgin Mary from first name Bible opens to* [*but has hard time living up to name*]), A1337.9* (*Origin of palsy*), P483.1* (*Conjurer uses black magic to cause death*), X1209* (*Mules always run away whenever something rattles in wagon*), W125.6* (*Child eats millions of flies*), J1518* (*When asked why bull won't return, servant replies, "Old George is dead"*), X749* (*Widower uses barrels of lemonade to seduce women*), V65.4.2* (*Repeated sermons part of extended funeral*), V65.4.1 (*Funeral song sung over dead*), K171.10* (*Insurance men make profits from selling policies during funeral services at grave*), K1925* (*Trickster boys switch sleeping babies during church service*), T249.3* (*Husband of deserting wife is told she is not frozen to farm work*), X939.1* (*Remarkable biter*).

51. Hunting the Christmas Baby

William V. Bunker, who knew the ways of Madison folks, told me this story in 1959. Its central motif is V211.1.8.4* (*Christ is hunted as the Baby each Christmas*).

52. The Mummy Lover

This well-known legend, which exists in both oral and printed versions, came from George Key, a taxi driver I met in Key West in 1949, when he was forty-nine years old. George had lived all his life in Key West.

The central motif is T211.4, *Spouse's [lover's] corpse kept after death.*

53. Foreknowledge of Death

Born in Bradenton, Florida, in 1921, and later a resident of Orlando, Nancy N. Rood told me in 1949 about this experience she said she had in Jacksonville during the Second War. It features Motifs D1812.5.1.2 (*Bad dream as evil omen*) and D1813.1 (*Dream shows events in distant place*).

54. Tall Tales

These anecdotes were part of the repertoire of Lewis D. Hughen, whom I knew during the spring of 1949. Born in Milton, Florida, and proud of being a Florida Cracker, Lewis lived in Pensacola and Tallahassee for several years. After completing graduate studies at the Florida State University, he became an enthusiastic teacher of folklore in North Florida schools and colleges.

Included among the older traditional stretchers from the United States, which I collected in "From Reality to Fantasy: Opening-Closing Formulas in the Structures of American Tall Tales," these tales are arranged here by their subjects since, as far as I know, they have not clustered around a central hero in Florida as they have in other areas (Pecos Bill, Febold Feboldson, and many others).

Tall tales are generally concerned with familiar subjects like weather, fishing, hunting, bird dogs, fast runners, and snakes. Some of these are localized to the Florida setting (for examples, g, n, and s). The following is a list of their central motifs.

a: X1623.3 (*Lie: flame freezes*). b: X1623.2 (*Lie: words freeze*). c: X1633.2* (*Lie: weather so hot that it parched peanuts, cooked syrup in cane, and made peanut candy*). d: X1633.1 (*Lie: weather so hot that corn pops in the field, animals freeze to death thinking it has snowed*). e: X1643.2* (*Lie: weather so dry that fish kick up dust in river*). f: X1321.3.3* (*Snake fed moonshine to make it cough up frog; returns with another frog*). g: X1318* (*Minnow fed liquor brings large fish in its mouth to fisherman*). h: X1110 (*The wonderful hunt*). i: X1130.4* (*Hunter shoots game so far away that he has to put salt on bullet to keep game from spoiling until he reaches it*), X1122.2.1* (*Lie: hunter shoots pits from peaches lined up on tree*), X1125* (*Hunter shoots opponent's bullets down as they are fired at him*). j: X1611.1.1* (*Big wind blows up cow like a balloon*). k: X1645.2.2* (*Lie: heavy rain flows through bunghole and bursts barrel*). l: X1215.8.1* (*Dog holds covey of birds in gopher hole and lets them out one at a time for hunter to shoot*). m: X1215.8.2* (*Dog catches coon to fit size* *of hide-stretching board*). n: X1286.2.1* (*Mosquitoes decide to eat man at once before big mosquitoes can take him away from them*). o: X1286.2.2* (*Mosquitoes eat horse; then pitch horseshoes to see who will get horse's owner for dessert*). p: X1124.5* (*Hunter holds deer by horns until his bullet reaches it*). q: X1796.2* (*Train moves so fast that man sticking his head out of a window to kiss woman kisses an animal in another state*). r: X1321.3.2* (*Two hoop snakes swallow each other's tails*). s: X1645.2* (*When well dries up, it is cut into postholes for sale*).

Many of these motifs are mentioned along with others in chapter 2, "The Rise of Native Folk Humor," in Richard Dorson's *American Folklore*, where an excellent bibliography on humorous tales can be found on pages 288–91.

Several variants of these Florida tall tales appear in Lowell Thomas's *Tall Stories: The Rise and Triumph of the Great American Whopper:* "Cold Light," pp. 148–49 (variant of a); "Chilled Vocabulary," pp. 152–54 (variant of b); "The Mule and the Popcorn," pp. 162–66 (variant of d); "A Hot Time in the Old Town," pp. 166–67 (variant of e); "The Convivial Snake," pp. 36–41 (variant of f); "The Minnow and the Moonshine," pp. 34–36 (variant of g); "Perhaps It Was Daniel Boone," pp. 74–77 (variant of h); "The Good White Tornado," pp. 167–69 (variant of j); "Man's Best Friend," pp. 92–94 (variant of l); "Skeeters Are Hearty Eaters," pp. 110–11 (variant of n and o); "The Ladies, God Bless Them," pp. 126–27 (variant of r).

55. More Stretchers

These tales date from the 1950s. Tales a, b, and c came from Martin Sapp, a storekeeper in Winter Beach, Florida. Tales d, e, and f, from the backwoods of Taylor County, belong to the repertoire of Warren Donaldson, who said he was "born a liar, and I've been one ever since." The tales of the pumpkin, the deer, and the sons are among his best. They were told to me by Clara Williams of Winter Beach in 1951.

Motifs in Mr. Sapp's tales were: a, X1286.1.7.1* (*Mosquito big enough to fence in ten acres of land with its bones; skull used to house corn grown*). b, X1411.1.1 (*Lie: large watermelon*). c, X1286.1.4 (*Large mosquitoes fly off with kettle*).

Motifs in Mr. Donaldson's tales were: "The Big Pumpkin," X1411.2 (*Lies about large pumpkins*). "The Peachy Deer," X1130.2 (*Fruit tree grows from head of deer shot with peach pits*). "The Three Sons," X1215.11.1* (*Split dog kills various animals, but is good as new when put back together*).

Variants from Lowell Thomas, *Tall Stories:* "The Triumph of New Jersey," pp. 122–23 (variant of a); "The Flying Kettle," pp. 101–5 (variant of c); "The Cherry Tree," pp. 86–88 (variant of e).

56. The Connoisseur's Sensitive Taste

This instance of the dupe who unconsciously happens to say the right thing came to me from Inez Walker of Wakulla in 1949. Its motif is

J1319.2*, *Boastful wine tester, when blindfolded, says there will never be any demand for this drink [really creek water]*.

57. The Right Platform for the Republican Party

The insulting phrase as a political trick is beautifully illustrated in this anecdote, told by Gerry Gordon as he heard it from Charlton Pierce, a Tallahassee lawyer, in 1959. Its motif is J1369.6* (*Politician says manure spreader is the best platform to speak of evils of Republican party*).

58. Putting His Foot in His Mouth

This joke came from Sidney Grovenstein of West Palm Beach, who studied his family's tales from 1950 to 1954. It is a good example of the trickster tricking himself. It includes Motifs J1510 (*The cheater cheated*) and K1697* (*Tramp says he is a good Catholic because his mother was a nun and his father was a priest*).

59. Courting Problems

This joke came from Samuel Sampson, who also contributed other tales in this collection. He was a black preacher with a good sense of humor enjoyed by his Leon County friends. The parents in the story figure as the tricksters because they did not like the young men courting their daughters, yet the tale turns back on itself when one lover gives himself away. When Mr. Sampson told this tale, he said he suspected the parents had put the chairs in the way for the intruders to stumble over. Its motif is J1511.21* (*Stealthy lover bumps into chair and says, "Just another damned cat!"*).

60. Golden Wedding Anniversary

This anecdote from Tallahassee was included in Elizabeth Thomson's recollections published in the *Guide to North Florida* (September–October 1981, p. 18). It exemplifies the long-suffering wife finally getting her revenge, Motif J1545 (*Wife outwits husband*).

61. Stolen Camellias

My father, Joseph R. Reaver, lived in Tallahassee during the 1960s, when he became acquainted with Dr. Ralph Eyman through their membership in the First Presbyterian church and their mutual enthusiasm for growing camellias.

This episode circulated among many friends of Dr. Eyman, who had a fine sense of humor. The story is doubly amusing because Dr. Eyman was the last person in the world to be thought of as a thief. Circumstances sometimes cast one in the role of a trickster without one's knowing it.

The story has continued to circulate in Tallahassee for some twenty years or more. It was retold in the *Guide to North Florida* (September–October 1981, p. 18) by Elizabeth Thomson, a retired university professor. Its motif is J1649* (*Mistaken act: man picking up discarded flowers is told, "So you're the one who's been stealing flowers from my cat's grave!"*).

62. The Stolen Bus Ticket

This jest with its trick ending came from Helen and Dorothy Osborn in the fall of 1950. These sisters liked to tell an apparently serious story that would turn into something foolish. The listener is the butt of the joke played by the storyteller, who is the trickster. This one includes Motifs X1780 (*Absurdity based on the nature of the object*), Z10.2 (*End formulas*), and Z13 (*Catch tales*).

63. The Good Baptist

Jo Campbell, who told me this tale in 1955, was born in St. Joseph, Missouri, in 1937. She heard it from her father, I. L. Campbell, an engineer living in Panama City, Florida. Its motif is V386* (*Baptist joins Methodist church just before his death since he cannot stand to see a Baptist die*).

64. Traditional Rivals

This jest was told to me in 1950 by Mildred Winfield of Ocala, who said, "You know, everyone here understands that any rain cloud happening to pass over Florida is an empty coming back from California."

The story pokes fun at strenuous labors of treasure seekers. Its motif is K2389* (*Man gets treasure by wearing tattoo "California is better than Florida," which no shark can swallow*).

Overlapping themes occur in Lowell Thomas's *Tall Stories*:

"Tall Tales of Florida Fish," pp. 52–54 (well-trained fish); and "California Climate," pp. 175–77 (California air from bicycle tires revives dying persons).

65. The Gluke Maker

During the Second World War, satire circulated in numerous tales spun out to nearly intolerable lengths for the purpose of poking fun at the government's elaborate scientific experiments demanding huge financial support. Top-secret code names such as *clish, gluke, gush,* and the like further made these experiments tempting objects for ridicule.

I found variants of this joke throughout Florida's cities, from Miami to Pensacola. This version came from Helen Atwater of Chattahoochee in 1949. Its central motif is K110 (*Sale of pseudo-magic objects*).

66. Self-Burial

Calvin C. Phillips belongs to the large number of Pennsylvania Germans who settled throughout Florida, especially in the early twentieth century. He is remembered for the peculiar architectural monuments he left behind (see *Tallahassee Magazine*, Winter 1981, pp. 45–46).

True or not, his story suggests such motifs as E334.1 (*Ghost haunts scene of former misfortune or crime*), E334.2 (*Ghost haunts burial spot*), F788 (*Remarkable bier*), and F852 (*Extraordinary coffin*).

Two of the best collections of ghostly tales from particular states are Louis C. Jones's *Things That Go Bump in the Night* for New York ghosts (New York, 1959) and Ruth Ann Musick's *The Telltale Lilac Bush and Other West Virginia Ghost Tales* (Lexington, Kentucky, 1965). Canadian ghost legends appear in Helen Creighton's *Bluenose Ghosts* (Toronto, 1957). Jones interprets tales of the horrible and macabre in "The Ghosts of New York," *Journal of American Folklore* 57 (1944): 237–54. Rosalie Hankey covers California ghosts in *California Folklore Quarterly* 1 (1942): 155–77.

67. Buried Alive

This horror story from Mrs. I. L. Campbell of Panama City (told to me in 1955) resembles the classic, archetypal form of the story of live burial. She mentions that such a story can occur only in days before embalming; in this way it differs from the more recent sort of terrible tale that reverses the use of embalming so that it causes unexpected death to a living person.

Motifs include F1041.1.11 (*Death from fear*), F1041.17 (*Extraordinary result of fear*), N384 (*Death from fright*), and S123 (*Buried alive*).

I reported more recent urban versions in my article " 'Embalmed Alive': A Developing Urban Ghost Tale." Live embalmings are also discussed under stories of the "Poisoned Dress" in Jan Harold Brunvand's *The Choking Doberman and Other "New" Urban Legends*, pp. 112–14. A French literary treatment occurs in André Maurois's "La Maison," in *Toujours l' Inattendu Arrive* (Editions de la Maison Française, 1943).

68. The Living Corpse

Numerous stories of people being buried alive exist in Florida, as well as other parts of the United States. This version combines terror and comedy. It came from Jo Campbell, who retold it as she remembered it from her mother, Mrs. I. L. Campbell of Panama City, in 1955. Mrs. Campbell remembered it from her early years spent in Montgomery, Alabama.

Such stories originated in earlier times when embalming was not widely used. The theme of live burial appealed to Edgar Allan Poe, who used it to great effect in "The Premature Burial," in which a man is obsessed with fear that this fate will be his own.

The story includes Motifs E1 (*Person comes to life*), E121.1.3 (*Man sent back to earth by Death, for it is not yet his time to die*), E152 (*Body still warm restored to life*), E390 (*Friendly return from dead*), S123 (*Buried alive*).

69. Saved from Live Burial

As if to compensate for the tales of being buried alive, people like to circulate stories of miraculous escapes from this fate. Mrs. I. L. Campbell of Panama City, as in the previous note, told this burial tale to her daughter Jo in 1955.

Motifs are F1088.5* (*Happy escape from being buried alive*) and F950 (*Marvelous cures*).

70. The Tallahassee Witch

The intriguing aspect of this witch is that nobody knows the complete story of her life. The speculations about her are based on the appearance of her monument and its inscription together with the non-Christian manner of burial. The tombstone is built tightly against the rear stone wall to the east of the burial plot so that the body must face west. The plot, entirely surrounded by a low stone wall, is large enough for several bodies. On the south base of the tombstone the monument maker is identified as "J. F. Manning, Wash., D.C." All appearances indicate that a well-to-do family provided the plot and its elaborate material.

On the shaft of the monument the inscription tells us that Elizabeth Budd Graham was the wife of John Alexander Graham and the daughter of David C. and Florence J. Wilson, born October 19, 1866, married November 24, 1887, and died November 16, 1889, "a dutiful daughter, a devoted mother and a loving and faithful wife." Below this inscription the odd poem appears. The shaft of the monument is topped by a finial of feathers with a design of ivy leaves and the cross within a crown around the base of the finial.

The plot is the most frequently visited place in the old city cemetery. According to the caretaker I talked to in 1984, many persons ask him where to find the grave of the witch.

The most tantalizing question is: "Who wrote the poem that has given rise to so many contradictory feelings?" Is it conceivable that Bessie could have suggested some of these lines in an attempt to hint at the shadowy side of her life? Or did her husband or parents prepare this confusing poetic memorial?

Motifs associated with Bessie the witch are G273 (*Witch rendered powerless*), D1172.2 (*Magic bowl*), E481.2 (*Land of dead across water*), A672 (*Stygian river*), and G278 (*Death of witch*).

71. The Haunted Jail

The Tallahassee jail has been the subject of speculation for many years. After its inspection by Robert M. Boggs in 1981, the jail was condemned, and by the winter of 1984 it stood dismantled with all its windows and doors removed so that it appeared after dark to be an eyeless white monster lurking in its lonely valley beyond the state buildings on the hill above it. Now a new jail has been built.

Richard Winer and Nancy Osborn Ishmael give an account of the séance in the jail in *More Haunted Houses* (New York: Bantam Books, 1981), pp. 45–50.

Motifs that appear in the various reports about the jail are E280 (*Ghosts haunt buildings*), E275 (*Ghost haunts place of great accident or misfortune*), E422.1.11.4 (*Revenant as skeleton*), E291.2.1 (*Ghost in human form guards treasure*), N517.1 (*Treasure hidden in secret room*), and E293 (*Ghosts frighten people [deliberately]*).

An elaborate account of another southern jail afflicted by similar ghosts occurs in Jeanne de Lavigne's *Ghost Stories of Old New Orleans* (New York: Rinehart and Co., 1946), pp. 179–91, "The Ghosts of Carrollton Jail."

72. The Music Lover

When she told this story, Flora Stout said she heard that the music student had lived in Montgomery, Alabama, and the strange visitor had escaped from the Raiford Prison Farm in Florida. In other versions, the frightening man escaped from an insane asylum. The story has turned up in north Florida (where Flora was living in Pensacola from 1930 to 1951), Alabama, and Georgia; in the early 1950s I heard a similar version from Joanne Hempstead, who said she heard it in Thomaston, Georgia.

Motifs are E384 (*Ghost summoned by music*), D2161.3.8.2* (*Insane man's rage quieted by music*), F959.1 (*Madness miraculously cured*), F1041.7 (*Hair turns gray from terror*).

73. The Face on the Windowpane

The belief in an indelible impression left by a face on a windowpane has wide circulation. Mrs. I. L. Campbell told an especially exciting version in Panama City in 1955, in which the face returns to successive windowpanes, no matter how many are replaced, until the window is covered with the picture.

Motifs are F782 (*Extraordinary doors and windows*), F968 (*Extraordinary thunder and lightning*), and D992.3 (*Magic face*).

It is worth noting that while in some versions lightning causes the impression of the face on the glass, here it only kills the girl; then her face mysteriously appears on the windowpane.

Unnatural effects on glass may stem from a misunderstanding of technology, dating back to the beginning of photography with its glass plates and flashlight powder producing images that many people could not understand. Speculations about these amazing effects were blended with popular beliefs in ghosts or other spirits. There are stories not only about ordinary people but about murder victims, criminals, and

Christ leaving images on glass. Brunvand mentions the image on glass in *The Choking Doberman* (p. 200), but the subject is more fully treated in Barbara Allen's "The 'Image on Glass': Technology, Tradition, and the Emergence of Folklore."

74. Room for One More

Hettie Syfrett from Wausau, Florida, recalled this fearful tale in 1948. It is a widely circulated story. In the version published by Bennett Cerf in *Famous Ghost Stories* (pp. 351–53), the intended victim travels from New York City to the country estate of distant relatives "in Carolina," where she has a vision of a hideous white-faced coachman who tells her he has room for one more in his black coach. The spectral appearance returns the next night. After returning to New York, she is about to enter an elevator when she sees the same specter operating the elevator; she draws back just in time to avoid the crash that crushes the other passengers to a pulp.

The story includes Motifs E279.2 (*Ghost disturbs sleeping person*), E200 (*Malevolent return from the dead*), E275 (*Ghost haunts place of great accident or misfortune*), and E299.1 (*Ghost causes machinery to run unattended*).

75. The Fraternity Initiation

Told to me by the Osborn sisters of Miami in 1950, this tale is widely known as a campus thriller, in more or less elaborate versions depending on the imagination of the storyteller. One of the most fully developed variants appears in "The Current Crop of Ghost Stories," in Bennett Cerf's *Famous Ghost Stories* (pp. 353–56). The Osborn version seems like an abbreviated summary of the longer story.

The story contains Motifs H1411 (*Fear test: staying in haunted house*), N384.4 (*Fraternity initiate dies of fright*), M370.1 (*Prophecy of death fulfilled*), and Q556.10 (*Curse for murder*).

76. Effects from a Skylight

This horror story is an example of the lore that circulates on college campuses. Since details of place are indefinite, the scene could be anywhere during a college Christmas vacation. Nancy Rood attended the Florida State University, but she related these events in 1949 as though they had happened on another campus.

Motifs are J1790 (*Shadow mistaken for substance*), F1041.17 (*Extraordinary result of fear*), K950 (*Various kinds of treacherous murder*), S116.4 (*Murder by crushing head*), W121.8 (*Illness from fear*).

77. The Cadaver Arm

Told by the Osborn sisters of Miami in 1950, this tale is typical of anecdotes told to scare college students.

Motifs are E422.1.11.3 (*Ghost as hand or hands*) and N384.0.1.1 (*The cadaver arm*).

78. The Wife Who Wouldn't Wear Pants

Thomas Hays, born in DeLand, Florida, in 1920, heard this tragicomic tale of domestic strife while he was living in Tallahassee in 1949.

It is constructed of Motifs E235 (*Return from dead to punish indignities to corpse or ghost*), E419.7 (*Person with missing bodily member cannot rest in grave*), F636.3.1* (*Remarkable pumper of water*), and Z181.2* (*Nudity: wife who will never wear pants*).

79. White Visitor to Cemetery

Hettie Syfrett, born in 1927 in Wausau, Florida, south of Chipley, heard this tale from friends in the Panhandle region, where she lived from 1948 to 1950. The story belongs to the category of the rationalized ghost story. Its central motif is E422.4.3 (*Ghost in white*).

80. The Bewitched Cow

This tale came from Barbara Hudnall's mother, who had heard it in Georgia from an elderly black. Mrs. Hudnall told it in Marianna, Florida, in 1949.

Motifs include E761.1.10 (*Life token: milk becomes bloody*) D457.2 (*Transformation: milk to blood*), D2083.2.1 (*Witches make cows give bloody milk*), G273.6 (*Witch rendered powerless by drawing blood from her*), and D1741.2.1 (*Drawing witch's blood annuls her spells*).

81. Anamoses and Truenina

This kind of tale with song (*cante-fable*) sings in the listener's ears through its music and its rhythmic language. Nancy R. Rood, who lived in Bradenton, had a grandfather living in Wimauma, Florida, after spending his youth in Alabama and Georgia. In the summer of 1949 he told her this story about the two marvelous dogs.

Motifs are D113.1 (*Werewolf*), D421.1 (*Transformation: wolf to object*), D610 (*Repeated transformation*), K606 (*Escape by singing song*), D1384.5 (*Song as protection on journey*), D1275 (*Magic song*), D478 (*Water changed to other substance*), and D492 (*Color of object changed*).

82. Respect for Ghosts

This string of tales told to prove that ghosts exist and should be respected was told in 1950 by Samuel Sampson, a black storyteller from Leon County, Florida.

Motifs include N384.2 (*Death in the graveyard: person's clothing is caught*), N538 (*Treasure pointed out by supernatural creature*), E545.12 (*Ghost directs man to hidden treasure*), V67.3 (*Treasure buried with the*

dead), E632.1 (*Speaking bones of murdered person reveal murder*), E412.3
(*Dead without proper funeral rites cannot rest*), E235.2 (*Ghost returns to demand proper burial*), E275 (*Ghost haunts place of great accident or misfortune*), and E279.1 (*The ghost haunts outside at night in human shape*).

83. Specters, Spirits, and Souls

Some "ghost" tales are told as proof of the existence of immortal souls in the Christian religion; for the believer, the appearance of spirits witnesses to the unity between heaven and earth. Born in Falfurrias, Texas, in 1937, Arthur Moore had lived in DeFuniak Springs, Florida, before coming to Tallahassee. While he was living in Tallahassee during the summer of 1958, Arthur became acquainted with several black residents who told him accounts of their varied experiences with spirits. I collected their stories from him in 1958.

Motifs are E495.3* (*Marriage to dead fiancé*), E545.12 (*Ghost directs man to hidden treasure*), E415.1.2 (*Return from dead to uncover secretly buried treasure*), E412.3 (*Dead without proper funeral rites cannot rest*), E415.4 (*Dead cannot rest until money debts are paid*), E310 (*Dead lover's friendly return*), E421.1.1 (*Ghost visible to one person alone*), E410 (*The unquiet grave*), E361 (*Return from dead to stop weeping*), E419.10 (*Concern of ghost about belongings of its lifetime*), F642 (*Person of remarkable sight*), F642.7 (*Person of remarkable sight can see the soul*), E422.1.1 (*Headless revenant*), E415.5* (*Dead cannot rest until room of death is changed*), E421.3.6.1* (*Ghost as huge white dog*), E423.1.1 (*Revenant as dog*), E423.2.2 (*Revenant as rabbit [hare]*), E421.3.8* (*Ghost as white rabbit*), E722.1.2.1* (*Soul as good and evil entity*), E702 (*Composition of soul*), E707 (*Person with more than one soul*), E721.5 (*Wandering soul assumes various shapes*), E750.1 (*Souls wander after death*), E754.1.5 (*Condemned soul released by God*), E756 (*Person sees his own wraith*), E422.1.11.2 (*Revenant as face or head*), E756.1 (*Devils and angels contest for man's soul*), E755.2 (*Souls in hell [Hades]*), G303.1.1 (*The devil originates from God*), E521.2 (*Ghost of dog*), E730.1 (*Souls of animals*), E731.1 (*Soul in form of dog*), E754.5 (*Souls carried to heaven in chariot of light*), E722.2.10.1 (*Chariot of gods bears astral bodies of dead to heaven*), F66.1 (*Journey to upper world in chariot*).

84. The Roasted Cat

This story of the inexperienced user of a microwave oven is a well-known joke. Among others, Ann Durham, an executive secretary in the English Department at the Florida State University, called my attention to its wide currency in Tallahassee by the fall of 1982. This summary version is my own.

Jan Harold Brunvand (*The Choking Doberman*, pp.151–52) reports an unusual discussion of this tale in the magazine *New Jersey Monthly*, August 1982. During the conversation, writers and editors mentioned that the various victims of death in the microwave were a baby put in the oven by kids on LSD, a dog that blew up, a cat that had been caught in the rain, and a short-order cook whose insides had been gradually cooked by microwaves escaping a faulty microwave oven. Brunvand notes two other examples of this story, one about a cat (from the *San Francisco Chronicle*, January 30, 1983) and another about a dog (*Newsweek*, August 9, 1982), in *The Choking Doberman*, pp. 215–16.

Motif N339.18* (*Animal killed by drying its fur in microwave oven*).

Such a contemporary anecdote is often called a "foaf" story because it usually comes from "a **F**riend **O**f **A F**riend," an elusive source always remaining anonymous. Although this means of transmitting a tale is not new, it is frequently given as proof of the incident really happening, either by someone who swears he knows it must be true or by a newspaper reporter who heard it from a friend, or relatives of a friend.

Rodney Dale invented the term *foaf* for modern English stories he collected in *The Tumor in the Whale: A Collection of Modern Myths* (London: Duckworth, 1978).

85. The Concrete-filled Cadillac

True to form, this urban legend was reported from anonymous sources as a flourishing piece of gossip in "Those Folk Stories of Old Have Seen City Lights," *Tallahassee Democrat*, December 26, 1981.

It is further documented by Brunvand, who notes in *The Choking Doberman* (p. 220) a British version in which a Triumph convertible is filled with Readymix (see Dale, *The Tumor in the Whale*, p. 40). Brunvand also discusses it in *The Vanishing Hitchhiker*.

Columns dealing with such urban stories in the *St. Petersburg Times* are reprinted in Dick Bothwell's *BUM* (*Brighten Up Monday*) *Stories*.

Motifs are K2110.1 (*Calumniated wife*), T75.2.2* (*Rejected husband's revenge*), and X757* (*Husband thinking wife unfaithful dumps concrete on suspected paramour's car*).

86. The Choking Doberman

This tale seems to have made its Florida newspaper debut in the *Tampa Bay Star*, August 19, 1981. This article quotes a St. Petersburg policeman as saying, "I think it started at a cocktail party where a bunch of newsmen were" (Brunvand, *The Choking Doberman*, p. 8). Brunvand reports the earliest dated account from the *New Times*, Phoenix, Arizona, June 24, 1981. Its numerous versions are discussed in Brunvand, pp. 6–18.

Motifs are K951 (*Murder by choking*) and K1643 (*Animal strangled by victim which he tries to eat*). Perhaps a more precise new motif, K1643.1* (*Dog chokes on intruder's finger*), should be used.

87. The Dead Cat in the Grocery Sack

Rumors of this unlucky cat were reported in the *St. Petersburg Times* ("A Dead Cat Tells No Tales," October 2, 1972). Edna Boggs told me about its continuing popularity in Coral Gables, Florida, when I saw her at the annual meeting of the Florida Folklore Society at Ft. Lauderdale in 1985.

Brunvand (*The Choking Doberman*, pp. 216–19) cites two stories about thefts of a dead cat, both from the *Tri-Town Transcript*, Ipswich, Mass. (December 29, 1982, p. 6, and January 5, 1983, p. 6), showing the belief in a "true" story was changed to recognizing it as a folktale.

Motifs include N300 (*Unlucky accidents*), N380 (*Other unlucky accidents*), and N385 (*Unintentional injuries bring unfortunate consequences*). Perhaps the best new motif for this tale would be N339.19* (*Dead cat in grocery sack is inadvertently stolen*).

88. The Surprise in the Elevator

This version of the incident was told by my neighbor, Dr. Bart Wecksler, for the entertainment of neighborhood guests at a Christmas party in 1984. He had heard it while he was at the Ohio State University in Columbus, Ohio. I repeat it in my own words as I remember it.

The episode is traced through several variants in Brunvand, *The Choking Doberman*, pp. 18–28, where some reports from Ohio are cited.

The story certainly belongs under Motif N300 (*Unlucky accidents*), yet its implications vary from one account to another, with racial, sexual, or religious connotations; some emphasize Reggie Jackson's courtesy toward the frightened women.

89. Multiple Thefts

My wife, Grace Reaver, has heard such accounts related as warnings at meetings of various business and university women's groups in the 1980s. American versions are still circulating, and the story has a British variant in Jacqueline Simpson's "Another Modern Legend?" Letter to the Editor in *Folklore* 83 (1972): 339. (See also Brunvand, *The Choking Doberman*, pp. 193–94).

Motif K301.1.1* (*Master thief manages multiple thefts*) seems appropriate.

90. Treacherous Snakes

Rumors of such occurrences have been mentioned as though they were true events in Florida newspapers from time to time. A more objective treatment is in "Those Folk Stories of Old Have Seen City Lights," *Tallahassee Democrat*, December 26, 1981. Such tales clearly reflect the fears and anxieties of people living in metropolitan areas in an atmosphere of distrust.

Motifs are S111.8.1* (*Murder by poisonous snake eggs hatching inside electric blanket*) and S111.6.1* (*Murder by poisonous snake sewn in lining of coat*).

For a bibliography of Florida neighborhood stories of horrible events, see Brunvand, *The Choking Doberman:* "The Clever Baby-sitter," p. 77, from Charles A. Brown of Vero Beach in 1980 (putting the baby's head in the gas oven until it stops crying); "White Slavery," pp. 80–81, from Sara Rimer, *Miami Herald,* September 26, 1980, (attempting to abduct a young woman to white slavery in South America); "Government Legends," p. 195, from Dick Bothwell, *St. Petersburg Times,* n.d., comparing the "Price of Cabbage" memo (26,911 words) to such texts as Lincoln's Gettysburg Address (266 words) and the Declaration of Independence (300 words) to show extravagance in modern government; "Cord Lice," p. 202, from an undated clipping of an Associated Press release in Miami (reports on the cord lice in telephones and cable lice in computers that are known to leave nasty bites but can never be caught because they are invisible).

SELECTED BIBLIOGRAPHY

Aarne, Antti, and Stith Thompson. *The Types of the Folktale: A Classification and Bibliography*. Helsinki: Suomalainen Tiedeakatemia, Academia Scientiarum Fennica, 1961.

Allen, Barbara. "The 'Image on Glass': Technology, Tradition, and the Emergence of Folklore." *Western Folklore* 41 (1982): 85–103.

Balseiro, José Agustín, ed. *The Hispanic Presence in Florida*. Miami: E. A. Seemann Publishing, 1976.

Beck, Brenda E. F., Peter J. Claus, Praphulladatta Goswami, and Jawaharlal Handoo. *Folktales of India*. Chicago: University of Chicago Press, 1987.

Bloodworth, Bertha E., and Alton C. Morris. *Places in the Sun: The History and Romance of Florida Place-Names*. Gainesville: University Presses of Florida, 1978.

Boggs, Ralph S. "Spanish Folklore from Tampa, Florida." *Southern Folklore Quarterly* 1 (September 1937): 1–12; 1 (December 1937): 9–13; 2 (June 1938): 87–106.

Bothwell, Dick. *BUM (Brighten Up Monday) Stories*. St. Petersburg, Fla.: Great Outdoors Publishing Company, 1978.

Briggs, Katherine M., and Ruth L. Tongue. *Folktales of England*. Chicago: University of Chicago Press, 1965.

Brunvand, Jan Harold. *The Choking Doberman and Other "New" Urban Legends*. New York and London: W. W. Norton and Company, 1984.

———. *The Vanishing Hitchhiker: American Urban Legends and Their Meanings*. New York and London: W. W. Norton and Company, 1981.

Cerf, Bennett A. *Famous Ghost Stories*. New York: Random House, 1944.

Christiansen, Reidar Thorwald. *Folktales of Norway*. Chicago: University of Chicago Press, 1964.

Dégh, Linda. *Folktales of Hungary*. Chicago: University of Chicago Press, 1965.

Dorson, Richard M. *American Folklore*. Chicago: University of Chicago Press, 1959.

———. *Buying the Wind*. Chicago: University of Chicago Press, 1964.

———. "King Beast of the Forest Meets Man." *Southern Folklore Quarterly* 18 (1954): 118–28.

———. *Negro Tales from Pine Bluff, Arkansas, and Calvin, Michigan*. Bloomington: Indiana University Press, 1958.

Douglas, Marjory Stoneman. *The Everglades: River of Grass*. Atlanta: Mockingbird Books, 1947. Reprint ed., 1974.

Eberhard, Wolfram. *Folktales of China*. Chicago: University of Chicago Press, 1965.

El-Shamy, Hasan M. *Folktales of Egypt*. Chicago: University of Chicago Press, 1980.

Espinosa, Aurelio M. *Cuentos Populares Españoles.* 3 vols. Madrid, 1946–47.

First Citizens and Other Florida Folks. Edited by Ronald Foreman. Tallahassee: Bureau of Florida Folklife Programs, 1984.

Georges, Robert A. *Greek-American Folk Beliefs and Narratives.* New York: Arno Press, 1980.

Greenlee, Robert F. "Folktales of the Florida Seminole." *Journal of American Folklore* 58 (1945): 138–44.

Groene, Bertram H. *Ante-Bellum Tallahassee.* Tallahassee: Florida Heritage Foundation, 1971.

Halpert, Herbert. *Folktales and Legends from the New Jersey Pines.* 2 vols. Ph.D. dissertation, Indiana University, 1947.

Hanna, Kathryn Abbey. *Florida: Land of Change.* 2d ed. Chapel Hill: University of North Carolina Press, 1948.

Hauptmann, O.H. "Spanish Folklore from Tampa, Florida." *Southern Folklore Quarterly* 2 (1938): 11–30.

Hurston, Zora Neale. Manuscripts of the Federal Writers' Project of the Works Progress Administration for the State of Florida, 1938.

———. *Mules and Men.* New York and Evanston: Harper and Row, Torchbook Edition, 1970.

Huss, Veronica, and Evelyn Werner. "The Conchs of Riviera, Florida." *Southern Folklore Quarterly* 4 (1940): 141–51.

Jahoda, Gloria. *The Other Florida.* New York: Charles Scribner's Sons, 1967.

Kennedy, Stetson. *Palmetto Country.* New York: Duell, Sloan and Pearce, 1942.

Lovecraft, H.P. "Imprisoned with the Pharaohs." In *The Doom That Came to Sarnath.* New York: Ballantine, 1971.

Massignon, Geneviève. *Folktales of France.* Chicago: University of Chicago Press, 1968.

Matschat, Cecile Hulse. *Suwannee River: Strange Green Land.* New York: Literary Guild of America, 1938.

Megas, Georgios. *Folktales of Greece.* Chicago: University of Chicago Press, 1970.

Morris, Alton C. *Folksongs of Florida.* Gainesville: University of Florida Press, 1950.

O'Sullivan, Sean. *Folktales of Ireland.* Chicago: University of Chicago Press, 1966.

Paredes, Américo. *Folktales of Mexico.* Chicago: University of Chicago Press, 1970.

Parsons, Elsie Clews. *Folklore of the Antilles, French and English.* Memoirs of the American Folklore Society 26 (1943).

———. *Folklore of the Cape Verde Islands.* Memoirs of the American Folklore Society 15 (1923), pt. 1.

———. *Folklore of the Sea Islands, South Carolina.* Memoirs of the American Folklore Society 16 (1923).

Perrault, Charles. *The Fairy Tales of Charles Perrault.* Translated with foreword by Angela Carter. New York: Avon Books, 1977. See *Histoires, ou contes du temps passé, avec des Moralitez* (Paris: Claude

Barbin, 1697): "Le Petit Chaperon rouge" ("Little Red Riding-Hood") and "Cendrillon, ou la petite pantoufle de verre" (Cinderella").

Pino-Saavedra, Yolando. *Folktales of Chile*. Chicago: University of Chicago Press, 1967.

Poe, Edgar Allan. "The Premature Burial." In *The Short Fiction of Edgar Allan Poe*, edited by Stuart and Susan Levine. Indianapolis: Bobbs-Merrill Company, 1976.

Ranke, Kurt. *Folktales of Germany*. Chicago: University of Chicago Press, 1966.

Raspe, R. E., et al. *The Adventures of Baron Munchausen*. New York: Pantheon Books, 1969.

Reaver, J. Russell. " 'Embalmed Alive': A Developing Urban Ghost Tale." *New York Folklore Quarterly* 8 (1952): 217–20.

———. "Folk History from North Florida." *Southern Folklore Quarterly* 32 (1968): 7–16.

———. "From Reality to Fantasy: Opening-Closing Formulas in the Structures of American Tall Tales," *Southern Folklore Quarterly*, 36 (1972): 369–382.

———. "Henry, the Pole-Vaulting Fish." *Journal of American Folklore* 61 (1948): 313–14.

———. "Legends of the King's Highway: Anecdotes from St. Augustine." *Southern Folklore Quarterly* 20 (1956): 225–39.

———. "P'noblums." *Journal of American Folklore* 62 (1949): 63.

Roberts, Warren E. *The Tale of the Kind and the Unkind Girls: AA-TH480 and Related Tales*. Berlin: Walter De Gruyter and Company, 1958.

Rooth, Anna Birgitta. *The Cinderella Cycle*. Lund, 1951.

Seki, Keigo. *Folktales of Japan*. Chicago: University of Chicago Press, 1963.

Smiley, Portia. "Folklore from Virginia, South Carolina, Georgia, Alabama, and Florida." *Journal of American Folklore* 32 (1919): 357–83.

Smith, G. Hubert. "Three Miami Tales." *Journal of American Folklore* 52 (1939): 194–208.

Thomas, Lowell. *Tall Stories: The Rise and Triumph of the Great American Whopper*. New York: Harvest House, 1945.

Thompson, Stith. *The Folktale*. New York: Dryden Press, 1946.

———. *Motif-Index of Folk-Literature*. Rev. ed. 6 vols. Bloomington: Indiana University Press, 1955–58.

Walker, Warren S., and Ahmet E. Uysal. *Tales Alive in Turkey*. Cambridge: Harvard University Press, 1966.

Willson, Minnie Moore. *History of Osceola County: Florida Frontier Life*. Orlando: Inland Press, 1935.

———. *The Seminoles of Florida*. New York: Moffat, 1920.

Winer, Richard, and Nancy Osborn Ishmael. *More Haunted Houses*. New York: Bantam Books, 1981.

INDEX OF MOTIFS

Motif numbers are from Stith Thompson's *Motif-Index of Folk-Literature*. An asterisk after a number indicates a new motif I have assigned to a narrative element in this collection. Column 3 contains the identifying numbers of tales and their corresponding notes, where the motif appearing opposite in column 1 may be found.

A. Mythological Motifs

Motif		*Tale and Note*
A15.2	Brothers as creators	22
A185.7	God prepares food for mortal	26
A541.2	Culture hero as god of agriculture	26
A672	Stygian river	70
A875.1	Navel of the earth	22
A1010	Deluge	23
A1021	Deluge: escape in boat (ark)	23
A1022	Escape from deluge on mountain	23
A1301	Men at first as large as giants	24
A1315.1	Why men became gray-headed	24
A1315.2	Origin of bald heads	24
A1331	Paradise lost	24
A1337.9*	Origin of palsy	50
A1420.2	Gods teach how to seek and prepare food	27
A1420.3	Creator of food items	27
A1423	Acquisition of vegetables and cereals	26
A1427.3*	Origin of Packenham's rum	28
A2216.1	Bear fishes through ice with tail: hence lacks tail	1
A2600	Origin of plants	26
A2611.0.5	Parts of human or animal body transformed into plants	26
A2816	Origin of smoke	34

B. Animals

B210	Speaking animals	5
B211.1	Speaking beasts—domestic	5
B754.7.3*	Snake's offspring born through mouth	34
B765.14.2*	Man overcomes snake's hypnotic stare by waving gun at snake	47
B857	Animal avenges injury	5

C. Tabu

C602*	Pact with snakes that if snakes never bite Seminoles they will never kill snakes	39

| C642.1* | Forbidden barrel of rum contains corpse | 28 |

D. Magic

D113.1.1	Werewolf	81
D213.4.1*	Transformation: man to Spanish moss	25
D342	Transformation: cat to person	7
D421.1	Transformation: wolf to object	81
D457.2	Transformation: milk to blood	80
D478	Water changed to other substance (or vice-versa)	81
D492	Color of object changed	81
D610	Repeated transformation	81
D799.4*	Disenchantment by sweeping disturbed ground	34
D992.3	Magic face	73
D1040	Magic drink	34
D1162	Magic light	48
D1172.2	Magic bowl	70
D1233	Magic violin (fiddle)	31
D1275	Magic song	81
D1322.2	Light moving toward cemetery as sign of death	48
D1384.5	Song as protection on journey	81
D1483.3.1*	Magic tree: when planted, will never die	34
D1487.3.1*	Tree magically protected against all efforts to kill it	34
D1515.4.2	Snake stone applied to snakebite absorbs poison	39
D1654.3	Indelible blood	42, 48
D1712	Soothsayer (diviner, oracle, etc.)	14
D1741.2.1	Drawing witch's blood annuls her spells	80
D1812.5.0.4	Rising smoke as omen	34
D1812.5.1.2	Bad dream as evil omen	53
D1813.1	Dream shows events in distant place	53
D1960.4	Deathlike sleep	43
D2063.5	Magic discomfort: continual breaking of wind	12
D2083.2.1	Witches make cows give bloody milk	80
D2161.3.8.2*	Insane man's rage quieted by music	72

E. The Dead

E1	Person comes to life	68
E121.1.3	Man sent back to earth by Death, for it is not yet his time to die	68
E125.4*	Resuscitation by uncle	43
E152	Body still warm restored to life	68
E200	Malevolent return from the dead	74

Motif		Tale and Note
E235	Return from dead to punish indignities to corpse or ghost	78
E235.2	Ghost returns to demand proper burial	82
E248*	Ghosts stop car motor so that car cannot enter cemetery	48
E275	Ghost haunts place of great accident or misfortune	71, 74, 82
E279.1	The ghost haunts outside at night in human shape	82
E279.2	Ghost disturbs sleeping person	74
E280	Ghosts haunt buildings	71
E281	Ghosts haunt house	7
E291.2.1	Ghost in human form guards treasure	71
E293	Ghosts frighten people (deliberately)	71
E299.1	Ghost causes machinery to run unattended	74
E310	Dead lover's friendly return	83
E332	Nonmalevolent road ghosts	34
E332.3.3.3*	Vanishing visitor, disappears walking backwards	34
E334.1	Ghost haunts scene of former misfortune or crime	34, 66
E334.2	Ghost haunts burial spot	66
E361	Return from dead to stop weeping	83
E384	Ghost summoned by music	72
E390	Friendly return from dead	68
E410	The unquiet grave	83
E412.3	Dead without proper funeral rites cannot rest	82, 83
E415.1.2	Return from dead to uncover secretly buried treasure	83
E415.4	Dead cannot rest until money debts are paid	83
E415.5*	Dead cannot rest until room of death is changed	83
E419.7	Person with missing bodily member cannot rest in grave	78
E419.10	Concern of ghost about belongings of its lifetime	83
E421	Spectral ghosts	45
E421.1.1	Ghosts visible to one person alone	83
E421.3	Luminous ghosts	48
E421.3.6.1*	Ghost as huge white dog	83
E421.3.8*	Ghost as white rabbit	83
E422.1.1	Headless revenant	44, 83
E422.1.6.2.1*	Revenant with only stumps for legs	45
E422.1.10	Dismembered corpse	7, 30
E422.1.11.2	Revenant as face or head	7, 83

INDEX OF MOTIFS

Motif		Tale and Note
E422.1.11.3	Ghost as hand or hands	7, 77
E422.1.11.4	Revenant as skeleton	34, 71
E422.4.3	Ghost in white	79
E423.1.1	Revenant as dog	83
E423.1.2	Revenant as cat	7
E423.2.2	Revenant as rabbit (hare)	83
E425.1.1	Revenant as lady in white	31, 48
E425.2	Revenant as man	48
E481.2	Land of dead across water	70
E495.3*	Marriage to dead financé	83
E521.2	Ghost as dog	83
E521.2.3*	Ghostly dog grows larger, but one ear stays small	34
E521.3	Ghost of cat	7
E521.6*	Ghost as white goat	34
E525*	Ghost as turtle, becomes smaller until it disappears	34
E539.1.2*	Bolted door blows open	34
E545.12	Ghost directs man to hidden treasure	82, 83
E632.1	Speaking bones of murdered person reveal murder	82
E702	Composition of soul	83
E707	Person with more than one soul	83
E721.5	Wandering soul assumes various shapes	83
E722.1.2.1*	Soul as good and evil entity	83
E722.2.10.1	Chariot of gods bears astral bodies of dead to heaven	83
E723.1	Person sees his own wraith	83
E730.1	Souls of animals	83
E731.1	Soul in form of dog	83
E750.1	Souls wander after death	83
E754.1.5	Condemned soul released by God	83
E754.5	Souls carried to heaven in chariot of light	83
E755.2	Soul in hell (Hades)	83
E756	Contest over souls	83
E756.1	Devils and angels contest for man's soul	83
E761.1.10	Life token: milk becomes bloody	80
E783	Vital head	16

F. Marvels

F66.1	Journey to upper world in chariot	83
F141.5*	Waterfall as location for state capitol	33
F513.1.2.2*	Person with diamond-filled teeth	47
F531.0.4	Giant woman	24
F531.1.6.3.2	Giant without hair	24
F543.1.3	Remarkably long, hooked nose	47

Motif		Tale and Note
F545.1	Remarkable beard	25
F548.0.2*	Short legs	29
F551.6*	Remarkably enormous feet	47
F628.1.2.3*	Man kills wild steer with one blow	47
F632	Mighty eater	47
F636.3.1*	Remarkable pumper of water	78
F642	Person of remarkable sight	83
F642.7	Person of remarkable sight can see the soul	83
F681	Marvelous runner	47
F700	Extraordinary places	33
F713.2	Bottomless lakes (pools, etc.)	34
F715.3	Rivers with marvelous underground connections	34
F718.13*	Spring originates from spot where vanished lovers stood	34
F725.10*	Stone with Andrew Jackson's name on it at bottom of lake	34
F782	Extraordinary doors and windows	73
F788	Remarkable bier	66
F852	Extraordinary coffin	66
F929.2.2*	Dinner guests swallow buzzard meat unwittingly	34
F931.5.1*	Shipwreck caused by misleading lights	30
F949.1	Animal sinks into earth	34
F950	Marvelous cures	69
F952.8*	Blindness cured by stroke of lightning	36
F959.1	Madness miraculously cured	72
F968	Extraordinary thunder and lightning	73
F1041.1.11	Death from fear	67
F1041.7	Hair turns gray from terror	72
F1041.17	Extraordinary result of fear	67, 76
F1088.5*	Happy escape from being buried alive	69

G. Ogres

G269.4	Curse by disappointed witch	11
G273	Witch rendered powerless	70
G273.6	Witch rendered powerless by drawing blood from her	80
G278	Death of witch	70
G303.1.1	The devil originates from God	83
G501	Stupid ogre	9
G514.1	Ogre trapped in box (cage)	8

H. Tests

H12	Recognition by song (music)	41
H221	Ordeal by fire	2

Motif		Tale and Note
H252.7*	Cursed courthouse clock never runs correctly	49
H602.3.1*	Cherokee Rose symbolizes loss of Indian girl belonging to Cherokee tribe	34
H1411	Fear test: staying in haunted house	75

J. The Wise and the Foolish

J17	Animal learns through experience to fear man	5
J216.7*	Pirate prefers drowning himself to being captured	30
J710	Forethought in provision for food	41
J1149.13*	Sheriff stays away from courthouse so he cannot detect arsonist (who will not pay taxes)	46
J1319.2*	Boastful wine taster, when blindfolded, says there'll never be any demand for this wine (really creek water)	56
J1325*	Drunk man is not any biblical character except Saul, who found his father's asses	47
J1369.6*	Politician says manure spreader is best platform to speak of evils of Republican party	57
J1510	The clever cheated	58
J1511.21*	Stealthy lover bumps into chair and says, "Just another damned cat!"	59
J1518*	When asked why bull does not return, servant replies, "Old George is dead"	50
J1545	Wife outwits husband	60
J1649*	Mistaken act: man picking up discarded flower is told, "So you're the one who's been stealing from my cat's grave!"	61
J1649.1*	Mistaken act: engineer congratulated on having train arrive at last on time says, "But this is yesterday's train"	34
J1705.5*	Stupid engineer	29
J1780	Things thought to be devils, ghosts, etc.	76
J1782.3.1*	Noise in woods thought to be ghost	45
J1791.3	Diving for cheese	4
J2341.1*	Nearsighted man thinks cows on road are spots on windshield	34

K. Deceptions

K18.3	Throwing contest: bird substituted for stone	9
K62	Contest in squeezing water from a stone	9

Motif		Tale and Note
K110	Sale of pseudo-magic objects	65
K171.1	Deceptive crop division: above the ground, below the ground	15
K171.10*	Insurance men make profits from selling policies during funeral service at grave	50
K301.1.1*	Master thief manages multiple thefts	89
K306	Thieves steal from each other	1
K312.1.1*	Thief hides in wagon; drops articles out	1
K319*	Thief induces dupe to attack bees; meanwhile he carries off honey	1, 2
K341.2	Thief shams death and steals	1
K354.2*	Trickster feigns hospitality but kills guests and takes their money	34
K371.1	Trickster throws fish off wagon	1
K401.1	Dupe's food eaten and then blame fastened on him	2
K419.11*	Blame for eating possum placed on owner whose mouth is covered with grease while he sleeps	2
K512.5*	Compassionate executioner: obtaining liquor in place of burning prisoner at stake	38
K581.2	Briar-patch punishment for rabbit	1, 6
K606	Escape by singing song	81
K735.5	Dupe tricked into well: left there	4
K741	Capture by tarbaby	1, 5
K752	Capture by hiding under screen	1
K891.5.4	Dupes deceived into falling over precipice	1, 3
K929.14*	Fox tells Wolf to keep tail in water to catch fish; water freezes and men kill wolf	1
K940	Deception into killing own family or animals	11
K950	Various kinds of treacherous murder	76
K951	Murder by choking	86
K1021	The tail fisher	1
K1025	Eating his own entrails	3
K1025.1	The fox suggests eating his own brains	3
K1025.2	Tiger persuaded to eat own eyes	1, 3
K1643	Animal strangled by victim, which he tries to eat	86
K1643.1*	Dog chokes on intruder's finger	86
K1697*	Tramp says he is a good Catholic because his mother was a nun and his father was a priest	58
K1725.2.1*	Hunter thinks churning water is thrashing monster	45

Motif		Tale and Note
K1813.3*	Man disguises himself as wife after her murder	32
K1854.2*	Corpse substituted for another so that it can go on the trip it always wanted	47
K1888	Illusory light	21
K1925*	Trickster boys switch sleeping babies during church service	50
K2110.1	Calumniated wife	85
K2150	Innocent made to appear guilty	2
K2389*	Man gets treasure by wearing tattoo "California is better than Florida," which no shark can swallow	64

L. Reversal of Fortune

| L54 | Compassionate youngest daughter | 12 |
| L330 | Easy escape of weak (small) | 1 |

M. Ordaining the Future

M110	Taking of vows and oaths	29
M341.2.0.1	Prophecy: death by particular weapon	29
M370	Vain attempts to escape fulfillment of prophecy	11
M370.1	Prophecy of death fulfilled	75
M398	Futility of weather prophecies	48
M412.1	Curse given at birth of child	11
M451.1	Death by suicide	34

N. Chance and Fate

N2.6.2	Daughter as wager	11
N6	Luck in gambling	36
N6.4*	Man never beaten at stud poker	47
N300	Unlucky accidents	35, 87, 88
N339.18*	Animal killed by drying its fur in microwave oven	84
N339.19*	Dead cat in grocery sack is inadvertently stolen	87
N380	Other unlucky accidents	87
N384	Death from fright	67
N384.0.1.1	The cadaver arm	77
N384.2	Death in graveyard: person's clothing is caught	82
N384.4	Fraternity initiate dies of fright	75
N385	Unintentional injuries bring unfortunate consequences	87
N511	Treasure in ground	14
N511.1	Treasure buried by men	30, 32

Motif		Tale and Note
N517.1	Treasure hidden in secret room in house	71
N517.2	Treasure hidden within wall (under floor) of house	34, 36
N525	Treasure found in chest (kettle, cask)	14
N538	Treasure pointed out by supernatural creature (fairy, etc.)	82
N619*	Child falling accidentally scares Indians	37
N827	Child as helper	12
N831	Girl as helper	12

P. Society

P170	Slaves	30
P201.2*	Feud between neighboring families	34, 35
P310.10*	Indian friend guards white children	34
P483.1*	Conjurer uses black magic to cause death	50
P673.1*	Footwashing for burial should not be allowed because man would not let anybody wash his feet when he was alive	47
P711	Patriotism	29

Q. Rewards and Punishments

Q2	Kind and unkind	12
Q411	Death as punishment	29
Q413.0.1	Threat of hanging	29
Q491.1.3*	Young man buried in tree after he is murdered to prevent his marriage	40
Q556.10	Curse for murder	75
Q597.3	Bees sting honey thieves	1

R. Captives and Fugitives

R12.5*	Ship captured by meeting of pirates	30
R211.3	Escape through underground passage	34

S. Unnatural Cruelty

S111.6.1*	Murder by poisonous snake sewn in lining of coat	90
S111.8.1*	Murder by poisonous snake eggs hatching inside an electric blanket	90
S113	Murder by strangling	11
S116.4	Murder by crushing head	76
S117	Death by dragging behind horse	1
S123	Burial alive	32, 67, 68
S133	Murder by beheading	30
S139.4	Murder by mangling with axe	42
S160.6*	Corpse mutilated by cutting off its head	28

Motif		Tale and Note
S162	Mutilation: cutting off legs (feet)	17
S183	Frightful meal	48

T. Sex

T24.3	Madness from love	32
T75.2.2*	Rejected husband's revenge	85
T211.4	Spouse's (lover's) corpse kept after death	52
T211.5	Man becomes hermit after his wife's death	32
T249.3*	Husband of deserting wife is told she is not frozen to farm work	50
T596.3*	Girl named Virgin Mary from first name Bible opens to (but has hard time living up to name)	50

V. Religion

V65.4.1	Funeral song sung over dead	50
V65.4.2*	Repeated sermons part of elaborate funeral	50
V67.3	Treasure buried with the dead	82
V115.4.1*	Agony bell rung to announce death	29
V211.1.8.4*	Christ is hunted as the Baby each Christmas	51
V253	Faithfulness to Virgin Mary, even if not to Christ, rewarded	29
V254.2	Ship in storm saved because of sailors' "Ave Maria"	29
V386*	Baptist joins Methodist church just before his death since he cannot stand to see a Baptist die	63
V400	Charity	47

W. Traits of Character

W111.1.7*	Man so lazy he would rather be buried alive than dig potatoes	47
W111.2.6	The boy eats breakfast, dinner, and supper one immediately after the other	1
W121.8	Illness from fear	76
W125.6*	Child eats millions of flies	50
W151.11*	Greedy preacher has congregation bow heads so that he can be first to reach shipwreck	30

X. Humor

X136*	Humor of lisping	47
X422	The corpse with his feet cut off	17

Motif		Tale and Note
X749*	Widower uses barrels of lemonade to seduce women	50
X757*	Husband thinking wife unfaithful dumps concrete on suspected paramour's car	85
X811.1*	Drunk man wakes up in cemetery and thinks he is first one up on Judgment Day	47
X932	Lie: remarkable drinker	48
X939.1*	Lie: remarkable biter	50
X942	Lie: remarkable carrier	48
X955	Lie: remarkable killer	48
X972	Lie: remarkable fighter	48
X1110	The wonderful hunt	18, 54
X1122.2.1*	Lie: hunter shoots pits from peaches lined up on tree	54
X1124.5*	Hunter holds deer by horns until his bullet reaches it	54
X1125*	Hunter shoots opponent's bullets down as they are fired at him	54
X1130.2	Fruit tree grows from head of deer shot with fruit pits	55
X1130.4*	Hunter shoots game so far away he has to put salt on bullet to keep game from spoiling until he reaches it	54
X1153	Lie: fish caught by remarkable trick	34
X1154	Lie: unusual catch by fisherman	21
X1209*	Mule runs away whenever something rattles in wagon	50
X1215.8.1*	Dog holds covey of birds in gopher hole and lets them out one at a time for hunter to shoot	54
X1215.8.2*	Dog catches coon to fit size of hide-stretching board	54
X1215.11.1*	Split dog kills various animals, but is good as new when put back together	55
X1286.1.4	Large mosquitoes fly off with kettle	55
X1286.1.7.1*	Mosquito big enough to fence in 10 acres of land with its bones; skull used to house corn grown	55
X1286.2.1*	Mosquitoes decide to eat man at once before big mosquitoes can take him away from them	54
X1286.2.2*	Mosquitoes eat horse; then pitch horse-shoes to see who will get horse's owner for dessert	54
X1301	Lie: the great fish	21
X1318*	Minnow fed liquor brings large fish in its mouth to fisherman	54

Motif		*Tale and Note*
X1321.3.2*	Two hoop snakes swallow each other's tails	54
X1321.3.3*	Snake fed moonshine to make him cough up frog; returns with another frog	54
X1411.1.1	Lie: large watermelon	55
X1411.2	Lies about large pumpkins	55
X1545	Lies about remarkable underground channels	34
X1611.1.1*	Big wind blows up cow like a balloon	54
X1623.2	Lie: words freeze	54
X1623.3	Lie: flame freezes	54
X1633.1	Lie: weather so hot that corn pops in fields, animals freeze to death thinking it has snowed	54
X1633.2*	Lie: weather so hot that it parches peanuts, cooks syrup in cane, and makes peanut candy	54
X1643.2*	Lie: weather so dry that fish kick up dust in river	54
X1645.2*	When well dries up, it is cut into postholes for sale	54
X1645.2.2*	Lie: heavy rain flows through bunghole and bursts barrel	54
X1710	Lies about numbers	36
X1780	Absurdity based on the nature of the object	62
X1796.2*	Train moves so fast that man sticking his head out of a window to kiss woman kisses an animal in another state	54
X1815.2	Lies about slow trains	34

Z. Miscellaneous Groups of Motifs

Z10.2	End formulas	62
Z13	Catch tales	62
Z18.1	What makes your ears so big?	10
Z46.1*	Continuous threats mount (Big Tor's feet, legs, eyes, hands, etc.)	10
Z181.2*	Nudity: wife who will never wear pants	78

INDEX OF TALE TYPES

Type numbers are from Antti Aarne and Stith Thompson's *The Types of the Folktale: A Classification and Bibliography.*

I. ANIMAL TALES (1–299)

Type		Tale and Note
1	The Theft of Fish	1
1*	The Fox Steals the Basket	1
2	The Tail-Fisher	1
15	The Theft of Butter (Honey) by Playing Godfather	1, 2, 6
21	Eating His Own Entrails	3
21*	The She-fox Declares She is Eating Her Own Brains	3
34	The Wolf Dives into the Water for Reflected Cheese	1, 4, 6
104	The Cowardly Duelers	5
121	Wolves Climb on Top of One Another to Tree	5
122Z	Other Tricks to Escape from Captor	1
135B*	Fleeing Fox Loses an Eye in the Briars	3
152A*	The Wife Scalds the Wolf	5
157	Learning to Fear Men	5
175	The Tarbaby and the Rabbit	1, 5, 6
210	Cock, Hen, Duck, Pin, and Needle on a Journey	2

II. ORDINARY FOLKTALES

A. Tales of Magic (300–749)

325	The Magician and His Pupil	7
326	The Youth Who Wanted to Learn What Fear Is	7
327A	Hansel and Gretel	8
327G	The Boy at the Devil's (Witch's) House	9
328	The Boy Steals the Giant's Treasure	9
333	The Glutton (Red Riding Hood)	10
410	Sleeping Beauty	11
431	The House in the Wood	12
465	The Man Persecuted Because of His Beautiful Wife	20
471	The Bridge to the Other World	13
480	The Spinning-Women by the Spring, The Kind and Unkind Girls	12
511A	The Little Red Ox	12
620	The Presents	12

C. Novelle (Romantic Tales, 850–999)

968	Miscellaneous Robber and Murder Stories	14

D. Tales of the Stupid Ogre (1000–1199)

1030	The Crop Division	15

Type		*Tale and Note*
1060	Squeezing the (Supposed) Stone	9
1062	Throwing the Stone	9
1065*	Contest in Chopping	16
1074	Race Won By Deception: Relative Helpers	15

III. JOKES AND ANECDOTES (1200–1999)

1310A	Briar-patch Punishment for Rabbit	1, 6
1561	The Lazy Boy Eats Breakfast, Dinner, and Supper One after the Other	1
1699*	The Coffin-Maker	17
1875	The Boy on the Wolf's Tail	21
1890	The Lucky Shot	18
1920B	The One Says, "I Have Not Time To Lie" and Yet Lies	19
1930	Schlaraffenland	20
1960B	The Great Fish	21
1960D	The Great Vegetable	20
1960F	The Great Kettle	20, 21